RATIONAL EMOTIVE THERAPY (REBT)
WORKBOOK

Table of Contents

Introducing Rational Emotive Behavioral Therapy (REBT)

A Human Empowerment Story

They don't teach this stuff in school. Our parents don't know it either. That's why we're never told about the superpowers of our minds or that we have control over how we think, feel and act. As a result, we tend to spend our lives feeling like the victim of circumstances. Life happens TO us. What we experience in life is determined by the outside world and we have little to no control over it.

Most people believe they're dealt a hand of cards at birth—including the parents card, the community card, the religion and life philosophy card, and a variety of other life circumstances that are outside of their control. Then, throughout their lives their mission on this earth is to play the cards they've been dealt. However, as life goes along, additional cards are added to their pile. The being bullied in school card, the breakup with your high-school love card, the addiction card, the failing college card, the getting fired card, the car accident card, the children card, the getting cancer card. They feel at the mercy of these cards because each new round they're dealt causes them to feel emotions, as well as causes them to act in certain ways, in reaction to what happens to them.

They want desperately to fit in, to be accepted, to be around good people who act appropriately and who love them. They spend most of their time trying to control the world around them in attempt at meeting their own needs. They do this by arguing to get their way, changing their jobs, moving to a new location, putting out the fires, buying the item they believe will finally make them happy. But no matter where they go it seems their problems follow them. No matter what they do, in the end they're still unhappy, unfulfilled, and angry.

It feels like life is constantly throwing things at them and putting obstacles in their way. Some people react to all of these cards by working frantically to try to control them—to stop more unwanted cards from coming. Other people begin to feel helpless and that they have no hope of feeling in control of their destiny, and so they give away their power and live their lives on autopilot, simply reacting to each new card that comes. Others choose to numb themselves to the whole thing.

You can imagine that as a result, most people are pretty stressed out and unhappy. This stress leads to a variety of mental and emotional problems, such as anxiety, depression, overwhelm, hopelessness, and even guilt and shame. Most people (ourselves included) have had those experiences where we feel like we suck at life, like we're failures at being human. With the invention of social media, now we can look at everyone else's perfect Instagram photos and feel even worse about ourselves. Everyone else seems to have received a much better hand! It's not fair!

Many people have sought professional help to cope with their emotional pain and dysfunction. However, most people suffer in silence. Part of the reason most people do not seek professional help for their mental or emotional suffering is that therapists and psychiatrists have a bad reputation, partially due to the over-prescription of psychotropic medication in modern times and partially due to the horrific treatment of mental health patients in the past.

The field of psychology, and specifically REBT, and CBT which is a related therapy, have given us humans a greater understanding of our own mind and powerful tools for taking back control of it.

What is REBT?

Rational Emotive Behavioral Therapy or REBT is like a human mind owner's manual! We are each blessed with the most powerful machine in existence—our minds—but we are never taught how to use it. With this course, that all changes!

There are two key reasons that it is so important to learn how to use the power of your mind:

The first reason you need to understand REBT and learn how to use your mind is that YOU WANT TO FEEL GOOD. No matter what your goal is or what you are trying to do, the true reason you are doing it is that you are seeking to experience some type of positive emotion. You want to feel happy, or at least you want to stop feeling terrible. This is the motivating force behind EVERYTHING you do. REBT teaches you how to feel more healthy, positive emotions.

The second reason it is so important to learn this stuff is that after you got beyond the child phase of life, where much of your life was outside of your control… once you entered adulthood… the truth is that YOU ARE RESPONSIBLE for many if not most of the cards you are dealt. REBT teaches us how to take control of our experience of life!

So, what exactly IS REBT? It's a process for changing thoughts, beliefs, emotions and behaviors.

R stands for rational, and it tells us the truth that most of the time, humans' thinking is pretty irrational. The good news is that when we think more rationally, our lives are better.

E stands for emotive, and it tells us that our emotions are affected by what happens, but not directly by what happens… it is our irrational thinking about what happens that causes our negative emotions.

B stands for behavioral, and it tells us that most of the time we act based on how we feel, and as we just said how we feel depends on what we think about what is happening around us.

T stands for therapy, of in this case it stands for teaching or training or techniques, and it refers to the fact that this is a process that can be LEARNED.

This course teaches the techniques and tools for taking back control of your life by learning how to direct your thoughts, emotions, and behaviors.

Not only does this course serve as a manual for how to use the full power of your mind, it will also provide evidence that yes, you CAN change your life. You can change how you feel. You can change your circumstances by choosing different behaviors. You can direct your own destiny. So, let's get started!

A Brief History of CBT/REBT and Psychology

Hundreds of years ago, doctors of the time were smart enough to recognize that the "mental health" problems people were having stemmed from the brain. But they were prehistoric enough to believe that drilling holes in a person's skull or other practices that are too disturbing to mention here would solve the problem. Obviously, this did not work.

Then, around the turn of the 20th century, a new field of science emerged… psychology. Early psychologists focused on psychoanalysis, which uses talk therapy to slowly work back in time or deeper into the patient's unconscious mind, revealing and confronting root causes of their emotional problems, which stem from within the patient's past. There was also an exclusive focus on mental illness and psychological dysfunction.

Then behaviorism was the next wave of psychology, and it focused on helping people change their behaviors rather than focusing on how they felt. The person's actions were the focus, rather than their inner experience.

Both the emotional and behavioral focuses helped, but they both largely ignored the way people THINK… and it turns out they were missing the most important factor to human psychology.

To most people today, the idea that our thoughts have a significant impact on our life experience seems like common sense, even if they don't understand how it works, exactly. But in the 1950/60s when Dr. Aaron T. Beck created CBT (Cognitive Behavioral Therapy) and Dr. Albert Ellis created REBT, they were the first to put the puzzle together that human thinking is a factor in emotional and behavioral problems. It was revolutionary!

"People are not disturbed by things but rather by their view of things." — *Albert Ellis*

Both Beck and Ellis recognized that the process of helping a client become aware of their underlying problems and unconscious issues didn't usually lead to a change in their behavior or lives. If it did work, it took a really long time. Dr. Beck noticed that his patients who struggled with depression had what he referred to as "automatic thoughts" that were often distorted and kept them in patterns of negative emotions and behavior. Dr. Ellis recognized that patients' thoughts stemmed from beliefs were often irrational and contributed to their emotional problems and behaviors. They both began experimenting with methods of helping clients change their thoughts and beliefs in order to change their emotions and behaviors. CBT and REBT were born.

This new perspective in psychology moved toward the underlying belief that the human mind can be trained and enhanced in order to produce happiness, fulfillment, and optimum performance, and away from the focus on mental disorders and dysfunction. CBT/REBT instead, recognizes the dysfunction of the faulty programming and seeks to reprogram it. Unlike other forms of psychotherapy used then, and today, CBT/REBT focuses on the "here and now" thoughts and belief and does not go digging back into the past looking for the root of emotional problems.

When Ellis was a young man, he had a fear of talking to women. He used himself as a test subject and for a month he visited a park nearby, where he made himself talk to 100 different women. The result was that as he continued exposure to the activity that he feared, his fear diminished. This behavioral self-experiment was so successful that he began using exposure therapy, as well as a variety of other behavioral processes, as part of his therapeutic process.

Over time, it was found that much of what was previously deemed "mental illness" was, in fact, simply normal human thought dysfunction and not mental illness after all. Mental illness was no longer seen as a permanent condition or defect, but rather a result of dysfunctional, irrational thinking patterns, which could be changed. What was revolutionary about this was the realization that by changing a person's thoughts, their emotional reactions could be changed, and therefore their behaviors could be changed as well. What this meant is that for the first time psychologists believed that people could change and fix mental illness.

The reason it seems like common knowledge today is that this discovery was the biggest shift in the understanding of how the human mind works—EVER. In the 60+ years since Ellis and Beck introduced these new concepts, psychologists have learned so much more about the human mind—all thanks to the door these two opened with this new perspective. It has become clear that the original viewpoints of psychotherapy, including that the human mind was primarily dysfunctional, are not true. In fact, the human mind is resilient and adaptable. It can unlearn bad habits and create permanent, dramatic change by learning new ways of thinking. We have more control over our thoughts, emotions, and behaviors than we ever could have imagined.

By the late 1990's, the positive psychology movement that grew out of these methods was in full swing. This concept has become the focus of all of the most influential major movements in modern psychology. The self-help and human potential movement, as well as the field of life coaching, are based on this notion of self-empowerment.

Knowing this, let's look back at that hand of cards we've been dealt. While there may be specific situations that life has placed in front of us, the truth that most people do not realize is that it is not what is on the card that impacts how we feel or what we do because of it. Rather, how we PERCEIVE what we are dealt is what causes our emotional reaction. And then our emotional reaction is what determines our behavior.

This can be a really hard idea to accept for many people. Many people have become very attached to the idea that the reason they are angry is because their boss snapped at them. The reason they failed the

6

test is because they spilled their coffee on themselves that morning, then they were late to school, and their teacher handed them a paper that they received a D on just before test time. And after all that, OF COURSE they were anxious… who wouldn't be? And, they're already a poor test taker, so under these conditions—with these cards they were dealt that day—it obviously would lead to failing the test, right?

The truth, however hard it may be to hear, is that they're wrong. None of those reasons is why they failed the test. They may have failed the test in part because they did not study and were unprepared. But more than anything, they failed the test because they do not know how to direct their own thoughts and emotions. The truth is that they could have had a better way of thinking about each of the cards they were dealt that day. They could have chosen to ease their own anxiety. They could have been more in control of how they responded to what was happening, but they didn't know HOW because no one ever teaches this stuff!

And the person who felt angry because their boss snapped at them? Think about this… do you really think their boss reached inside of their body and created the neurotransmitters or brain chemicals that produce the feeling of anger inside of that person? No, of course not. So, where did the anger come from? It came as the body's response to an angry THOUGHT. And, while it may seem reasonable or even normal for someone to think an angry thought when someone else snaps at them, the unfortunate (or I guess fortunate) truth is that it is 100% their CHOICE what they think about it and how they allow it to make them feel. Essentially, by reacting to their boss' actions with anger, they handed their boss the right to choose *their* emotional experience. They gave away their power.

So, if at this point you're ready to swallow the pill that your thoughts and emotions and the behaviors you take because of them ARE YOUR CHOICE… read on…

Here are a couple more examples….

It wasn't your boss who handed you the "you're fired" card… you handed yourself the "getting fired" card by slacking off at work.

It wasn't the other person or God that punished you with the "getting pregnant from a 1-night stand" card… you grabbed a hold of that card all on our own by choosing to having unprotected sex with a stranger.

The most important truth that must be accepted in order to finally be in control of our own lives is the fact that WE cause most of the cards we're dealt. And the reason we choose to act in the way that brings about these things we do not want is because we act based on how we FEEL. We feel angry that we didn't get a raise and so we slack at work… and we end up getting fired. We feel desperate for attention and approval and get tipsy at the bar and it feels so good to be wanted that we let our guard down and end up with a baby with a stranger.

Our emotions drive our actions. And the key here—hear this—is that our THOUGHTS drive our emotions.

If we learn how to think differently, we can learn how to control our emotions (more of the time). And if we are in more control of our emotions, we can more deliberately choose our behaviors. And if we choose our behaviors, we can stop choosing the ones that lead to the life circumstances that we do not want.

We don't expect you to understand how this works yet or even to believe it 100%. We don't expect you to be willing to accept your own personal responsibility for your life quite yet. But we anticipate that if you have never heard this before, you like the idea of being in control of your thoughts, emotions, and behaviors. And, if you already knew how this works to some degree, we're guessing you'd love to know HOW to do it!

Similarities and Differences Between REBT & CBT

What is CBT?

CBT stands for Cognitive Behavioral Therapy.

Cognitive refers to the process of learning and understanding through our experience, what we take in through the 5 senses, and what we think about all of it. Cognitive processes happen both consciously, meaning we are aware of them, and unconsciously, meaning they happen automatically, without our awareness.

Behavior refers to the way we act, which can happen deliberately (when we are aware of our cognitive processes) or reactively (when we are responding unconsciously to a situation).

The Core Principles of CBT

- Our thoughts create our emotions, which lead to our behaviors. We have the ability to control our thoughts, and therefore our emotions and behaviors.
- It is our perception of the situation, rather than the situation itself, that determines how we feel about it and how we react to it.
- Our perspective of a situation can change if we change the way we look at it, just like putting on a pair of glasses with a different colored lens or looking at an object from a different angle.
- When we have a negative interpretation of a situation, it causes a negative emotional reaction.
- Finding a positive viewpoint of a situation leads to improved emotional well-being.
- The actions we take are chosen based on what we think, and especially how we feel about a situation. Therefore, if we change the way we think, it changes our emotional state, which influences our decision making and leads to better decisions.
- When we change our negative thought process, improve our mood, and stop sabotaging behaviors, we are better able to meet our goals.

What is REBT?

REBT stands for Rational Emotive Behavioral Therapy.

Rational refers to the fact that most of the time, humans' thinking is pretty irrational. The good news is that when we think more rationally, our lives are better.

Emotive tells us that our emotions are affected by what happens, but not directly by what happens… it is our irrational thinking about what happens that causes our negative emotions.

Behavioral tells us that most of the time we act based on how we feel, and as we just said how we feel depends on what we think about what is happening around us.

The Core Principles of REBT

REBT also includes the core principles of CBT, with the following additional principles.
- You can't change the past, but you can change your beliefs about and because of the past.
- We all think irrationally, in predictable ways that are easily corrected.
- The meaning we assign a situation is both the biggest reason for our emotional reaction to it and our biggest opportunity for changing our thinking.
- Negative emotions can be both healthy and unhealthy.
- Self-acceptance is the antithesis of approval-seeking and the key to confidence.

- Releasing expectations and judgments of others is required to stop being angry and miserable.
- Accepting what is (including the parts you don't like) is the only way to take back your power.

Similarities and Differences

While CBT and REBT processes share much of their core principles, including that our behaviors and emotions are primarily caused by our attitudes, beliefs, and thoughts, there are a number of differences. The two processes focus on different aspects of cognition and have different goals. However, the two methodologies work extremely well when used together (like in this course), providing a complete process for evaluating and changing thoughts, emotions, and behaviors.

The main premise of CBT is that our thinking is distorted. This distorted thinking leads us to feel negative emotion. In order to shift the negative emotion, we need to identify the distorted thinking and shift our perspective to something more positive. By doing this, we shift our emotional reaction to the thought that we have about the situation.

The main premise of REBT is that our emotional disturbances are caused not just by the distorted thinking about a specific situation, but by irrational core beliefs.

The goal of both CBT and REBT is to change a person's emotional state and behavior, however they use different processes to achieve the desired outcome.

CBT focuses on THOUGHTS or changing the perception or interpretation of an experience. CBT is designed to help us manage our perceptions and interpretations, which can be distorted due to cognitive distortions or errors in thinking, as well as limiting beliefs. It teaches us how to become aware of and then teach us how to think more clearly, and positively. CBT helps us overcome negative, destructive thinking.

But it's not just positive thinking, it's logical, clear-minded, healthy thinking.

If you've ever made assumptions, jumped to conclusions, or made a situation worse than it was by worrying about the worst-case scenario, you have experienced a cognitive distortion.

Many of these faulty ways of thinking are obvious once you know they exist, but you don't notice them in daily life because almost all thinking happens automatically or unconsciously.

CBT also helps you tame the tormenting critical voice in your head and take your power back from others who have implanted limiting beliefs into your mind.

REBT focuses on thoughts too, but the emphasis is on changing the underlying BELIEF system that leads to the interpretation in the first place. The idea behind REBT is that by ripping the cause of the dysfunction out by the root—the core belief—it prevents the pattern of negative thinking, negative emotion, and negative behavior from continuing to happen.

Let's look at an example of how the two methodologies approach the same problem: Fear of rejection. Imagine you want to ask someone out on a second date but you're anxious about it. You tell yourself, well, she didn't smile or talk much on our first date. I don't think she's interested in me. You observed her behavior and made a judgment of what it meant but the truth is there are many other reasons that could be the cause of her behavior, other than her not being interested. CBT would call this cognitive distortion "mind reading" and would recommend you find a more positive way of looking at the situation. For example, you would identify that the assumption is just a cognitive distortion and you would then re-frame the situation by saying to yourself "I'm sure the reason she didn't smile or talk much is that she was nervous or maybe something else was going on in her life. Having a second date with her would allow us both to begin to feel comfortable with each other and get to know each other better." Changing the way you thought about it would change the way you felt about asking her on the second date, which would inspire you to be willing to reach out and ask her.

REBT would look further than the negative interpretation of the event. Instead, it would seek to identify the underlying reason you jumped to the conclusion that she wasn't interested in you. Why would your initial reaction be to assume she didn't like you? Because you're afraid of being rejected and you know that asking her out puts you at risk. What do you believe that would lead you to fear being rejected? The belief that you absolutely need her acceptance and that not getting it will be awful. It will mean you're a loser who will never find a relationship that lasts." And, at an even deeper level, there would be a belief that says I need to be accepted by everyone I deem important in order to be worthy as a person." This belief is of course irrational and extreme. However, it is beliefs like this that are at the root of all of our surface level irrational thinking or cognitive distortions. It's the reason for the assumption.

So, REBT would then help identify a more rational belief to replace the irrational one. For example, simply by changing the belief to say "I really want her to accept me, but I know that not everyone is going to like me and that's okay. It does not determine the outcome I will experience with other women." By letting go of the absolute need for acceptance, the fear of rejection is softened. At this point, the likelihood of your first assumption being that she doesn't like you diminishes, and even if you do think of it, you'll quickly remind yourself that it's not the end of the world if she rejects you.

Both methods have the desired effect of helping you feel better about the situation and take action toward your goal—which is to ask her out. But as you can see, the method of addressing the deeper level belief through REBT processes has a higher likelihood of creating long-term change.

Now that you have a general idea of the difference between the two, let's go over several distinctions that are important to understand about REBT.

Secondary Disturbance. In life, there are a variety of different things that disturb us, referred to as "disturbances" in REBT, that usually fall into two categories: a negative life experience or a negative emotional experience. It's important to note, however, that sometimes a life experience is not actually negative, however the person's interpretation of it makes it negative and causes a negative emotional reaction to it. CBT would look at this and say that the life experience simply is what it is, while the negative emotional experience is usually caused by the way that we think about the life experiences. REBT would acknowledge another layer of disturbance that happens when not only do you feel anxious because you are going to ask the woman on a date, you are afraid of feeling anxious while asking her or while on the date. You're anxious about being anxious. You're worrying about worrying. This is a secondary disturbance. Disturbing yourself about your emotional disturbance that you have about the actual, original life disturbance is too much for anyone to handle, which is why these secondary disturbances are often the major factor in severe depression, anxiety, and panic.

Another common secondary disturbance is guilt. Say you have anger problems and tend to snap at people you love. You then feel guilty for not controlling your rage. Another great example is someone who is working on overcoming his or her problems and feels like they're not making progress as fast as they think they "should" be able to. They have their problem and the stress it causes, plus the additional layer of emotional disturbance due to beating themselves up about it.

Often, in order to deal with the primary problem, the secondary disturbance must be addressed first. For instance, if a person cannot stop judging themselves for their nervous behavior, it makes it a lot harder for them to address the underlying problem because every time they're asked to reflect on their experience of anxiety, they feel anxious about it, which clouds their thinking.

Unconditional Self-Acceptance. CBT often focuses on improving a person's self-esteem by reinforcing their positive qualities and affirm their worthiness. When we teach about confidence (we have a whole course and book on it) we take it a step further. The truth is that trying to feel good about yourself by thinking you're good at something actually works against because if you need to believe you are good at something to feel good about yourself, failure or trying a new skills you're not good at yet will lower your self-esteem. True confidence is the belief that you are always able to learn and improve in any area, which is called having a growth mindset, which we'll talk about next.

REBT has a different method for improving self-esteem, which is unconditional self-acceptance. It encourages people to stop self-rating and instead accept themselves as imperfect human beings, regardless of their traits or behaviors or how others see them. Instead of rating their SELF, they would evaluate the results of their actions and behaviors and seek to change them, not because of a negative judgment of those behaviors but because of the undesirable outcomes because of them.

Later in this course, we'll get into more detail about unconditional acceptance.

Helpful Negative Emotions. Unlike CBT and most other cognitive therapies, REBT differentiates between self-destructive, inappropriate negative emotions and helpful, appropriate negative emotions. Anxiety, depression, and anger are examples considered unhealthy negative emotions, while sadness, sorrow, concern, or regret are considered healthy emotions. Later in this course we'll get into more detail about healthy and unhealthy emotions.

For example, if you feel intense sadness and grief when you lose a loved one, this is completely appropriate and healthy. However, if you feel anxious about arriving late to a meeting, this is unhealthy because the reason behind your anxiety is the fear of judgment and rigid thinking that says you must never be late to a meeting. While you may believe it seems reasonable to feel anxious if you're going to be late, the truth is that feeling anxious does not help the situation or make you get there faster. All it does is make your ride unpleasant and put you in a negative emotional state when entering the meeting. There is also a difference between moderate anxiety in that situation vs. panicking about it. The power of REBT and CBT is that they give you tools that help you learn how to manage these emotional reactions, making whether you feel anxious when you're late to a meeting or not a choice.

Irrational Thinking: How the Mind Works

Why We Think, Feel and Act How We Do

As we've established, REBT is based on the premise that our thoughts create our emotions and influence our behavior. The 3 aspects—thoughts, emotions, behaviors—interplay and influence each other, however the area where we have the most power is our thoughts because they are almost always the foundation of our emotions and the behaviors we take because of them. The good news, which is why REBT is so powerful, is that because we can learn to have greater control over our thoughts, we can have greater control over our emotions and our behaviors.

In every moment our brains are processing our experience taking in information through the 5 senses. When you experience anything in life, it is interpreted by your brain, which means in a split second your brain compares what it is taking in through your senses, which tells it what is going on in your experience, to everything else you've ever experienced. It's trying to make a snap judgment of:
1. What is going on
2. What does it mean
3. How should I feel about it
4. What should I do

The brain has evolved to rapidly interpret everything you experience and it's so good at it that you don't even notice it's happening. That is, until something happens that causes your mind to interpret a situation as negative. It chooses a perspective or belief about the situation that creates an emotional reaction in your body. It's unpleasant, so it's noticeable. Your body reacts to this emotion, which is actually caused by the thought triggering your body to release any of a number of brain chemicals, often referred to as neurotransmitters or endorphins or hormones. Your brain is like a chemical factory and there is a different neurotransmitter that is responsible for every emotion you can feel.

It all functions as it should. Something threatens you, your brain interprets, triggers the hormones that shoot throughout your body inspiring you spring into action. Someone tells you they adore you and you're flooded with feel-good chemicals. Our bodies and brain are amazing machines. But sometimes, these emotional reactions get out of whack with what's actually happening. You can feel anxious for no reason. Something small makes you furious. You're sad even when you're doing something that usually makes you happy.

What's happened is that your mind has learned a pattern of thinking that is faulty. Your brain is interpreting situations negatively, when they're not. Your mind is judging situations, or yourself. You have unconscious irrational beliefs impacting your perspective that you aren't aware of. Your brain was doing what it does best—trying to interpret your world in a way that protects you. Unfortunately, as you lived life, your brain got programmed by the world around you. Your thoughts were influenced by the actions of others. Your core beliefs were adopted from the beliefs of others. And because you weren't aware of any of this, your mind became trapped by its own faulty beliefs. Your thoughts run amok and you were never taught you to catch them.

It happens to everyone. Humans bodies and brains don't come with an owners' manual! But the good news is that the solution is simple. You can become more aware of this process. You can change your thought patterns and beliefs. You can reprogram yourself. You can become conscious of your unconscious thoughts and behaviors. You can choose to experience more positive emotions, and less negative ones.

You have this power to control your own mind—a power that has been withheld from you your entire life. And it's time to take your power back!

Let's Look at Emotions

The best place to start a discussion about how thinking works and impacts your life is to look at emotions. Let me ask you a question, should emotions be trusted?

Some people say, "You should always trust your emotions."

Other people say, "Feelings are irrational and can't be trusted."

So, which is it?

They're BOTH wrong.

Emotions and feelings are neither right nor wrong, accurate or not. Emotions are simply your body's reaction to what you are THINKING. Your belief system and other unconscious thoughts are happening on autopilot all the time, and cause emotions. That's why sometimes you have NO IDEA why you feel the way you do.

So, here's an example of why emotions are never either right or wrong... because they're just reacting to your thoughts...

Think about something that you really, really wish you had, but that you don't have.

You may feel unhappy because you don't have it, but that's not true. You are unhappy because of the THOUGHT of not having it.

Let me prove it to you:

Have you ever been happy while not having this thing you want? __Yes __No

If you didn't have it but you didn't care that you didn't have it, could you be unhappy? __Yes __No

If you didn't have it but were doing something else that kept you from thinking about it, such as going down a roller coaster, would you be unhappy about it? No.

You see, not having what you want doesn't make you feel bad.

Thinking about it does.

Where Do Emotions Come From?

Sometimes our unconscious mind and senses are picking up cues from our environment that trigger emotions, such as reading a person's body language or facial expression and having an automatic physiological response or sensing danger and having an automatic fear response. (By the way, to learn more about the fight-or-flight response that causes you to feel fear and anxiety, check out the Situational vs Psychological Fear section in the Developing Awareness section.)

However, most of the time it is NOT the outside world or the situation that is happening that causes our emotional reaction—it's what we're thinking. It is the mental filter that the situation passes through—aka, our interpretation—that then causes our emotional reaction to the situation.

Situation → Interpretation (Thought) → Emotion

The key to understand here is that research over decades on CBT provides evidence that we can have control over our thoughts. And if we have control over our thoughts, we can control our emotions. It may be challenging to do this, but it is a skill that can be learned. Here's the process:

Recognize Emotion→ Identify Thought → Change Thought → Change Emotion

Changing the Thought

Once you notice that a thought is happening it becomes conscious. Since you're aware of it, you can then choose to change it. Your mind automatically interpreted the situation, but now that you're paying attention to it you can choose a different interpretation—a different perspective. This is great news because when you change the way you look at things, the things you look at change. Even in the same situation or with the same facts, if you change your viewpoint, your experience of the situation will change. Here is an example: a man was visiting a friend's house and went into the kitchen to make some tea. He didn't find a tea kettle, and so poured water into a glass coffee carafe and placed it on the gas stove. He returned to the living room and minute later smelled something burning. He returned and found that the handle of the carafe had caught fire. He quickly put the fire out. He apologized to his friend and was feeling both embarrassed and guilty. His friend, however, was laughing and complemented him on his "fireman" skills. Same situation, different perspectives—and the result was completely different emotional responses.

Why this matters!

So, this matters because, of course, you want to feel better. If you change your perspective of a situation, you will change your emotional reaction to it. But it's even better than that!

You see, your emotions are the driving force for your BEHAVIORS because the decisions you make are based on how you feel. As you get better at being aware of your emotions and thinking, you'll be able to make decisions from a place of control—you might feel a certain way, but you'll use your cognitive processes to choose to act from a place of rational thought.

But if you're like most people, you're not at that place yet—at least not all the time.

So, here's where we are now:

$$\text{Thought} \rightarrow \text{Emotion} \rightarrow \text{Decisions} \rightarrow \text{Action/Behaviors}$$

The behaviors you exhibit and the actions you take are a direct result of your thoughts. So, if you are experiencing behaviors you don't like or have been doing things you aren't pleased with, your thoughts are to blame.

If you can't yet see the behaviors or actions you're doing that aren't serving you, look around at your life at the results you're experiencing. Have you been having any problems at work or in your relationships? Have you experienced anything unpleasant? Are there are things you want that you don't have? On the positive side, what aspects of your life have you managed to create that you want, enjoy, or love?

The reason I ask is because I'm going to take this cause and effect train one more step.

$$\text{Thought} \rightarrow \text{Emotion} \rightarrow \text{Decisions} \rightarrow \text{Action/Behaviors} \rightarrow \text{Results/Outcomes}$$

That's right, your behaviors and actions are what determine the results and outcomes you experience in your life—both the wanted ones and the unwanted ones.

By changing your thoughts, you can literally transform your life. Literally! So, let's dive into more about understanding how thinking works.

We All Think Irrationally! Yes, even you!

It's really easy to notice when someone else is thinking irrationally. What they say sounds illogical. It makes no sense! Even if you try to point out their error in thinking, they don't get it. They seem locked into their point of view, like they're blinded to the truth. It can be frustrating. But the truth is that the same thing happens to you.

Sometimes we all become blind to logic. Why? Because of the way our minds work.

Your brain's number 1 goal at all times is to keep you safe, and so it focuses on evaluating what is happening right now and predicting what is going to happen in the future. And while it is interpreting your world, it is very easy to misperceive or misunderstand situations that are happening around you or things people say to you. There are a variety of reasons for this.

First, at all times you are receiving limited information. One reason this happens is that literally we may just not know all of the facts. If you hear a loud bang outside, you cannot see what is happening and so may assume it's a gunshot when it's simply a car door. Your friend may sound irritated, and so you assume they're mad at you, but the truth is that you don't know what happened to them earlier in the day that may have them upset.

The other reason you are receiving limited information is because your brain is blocking out most of the information happening around you. The reason for this is because there are millions of bits of information going on around you all the time that could be picked up by your senses, however if you were consciously aware of it all you would go crazy. For this reason, your brain has a focusing mechanism called the Reticular Activating System that narrows down those millions of bits into 2,000 that are relevant to you. So, depending on whatever you're focusing on at the time, your brain picks up on data relevant to that topic. If you're at the airport and you've been talking to your sister about her baby, you notice all the babies crying as you walk through the terminal. If you are dressed in a suit and heading to an important meeting, you'll notice all of the other people dressed up who look like they're up to something important too. But your brain literally blocks out almost everything.

Next, whatever information your brain does have access to gets filtered through what is already in your brain. For instance, your brain takes this input and compares it to your beliefs to determine what you think about this information. It also searches through your memories to see what has happened in your past that in any way relates to this information, so it knows what it is. For instance, when a baby sees a four-legged creature that's hairy and his parent calls it a dog, the next time the baby sees a four-legged hairy creature he calls it "dog". But this time it's a cat. He does not know this because the only belief he had was that four-legged hairy things are called dogs. Now, imagine the baby had been bit by a dog. Now, the next time it sees a four legged creature the baby's brain is going to quickly evaluate this creature against the baby's belief systems and memories of past experiences, which of course will lead the baby to conclude this creature is a dog and dogs are something to be afraid of. The baby reacts to the dog with fear. The problem is that it's not a dog—it's an adorable bunny. The baby's thinking is irrational.

But the truth is, it is not that the baby is irrational—because based on what he knows it's actually quite smart to fear the bunny. This same exact processes is happening to all adults too, all of the time, in a split second. Irrational thinking happens because we have limited information about what is happening and we interpret it through our biased beliefs and memories of our experience, which are limited, not to mention memories are very often not accurate.

It's important to recognize that thinking irrationally does not mean we're doing anything wrong—just like the example with the baby, the truth is that our irrational thoughts actually DO MAKE SENSE based on our limited understanding.

The problem with irrational thinking is when it becomes problematic and negatively impacts our lives.

So, when we talk about irrational thinking, we are specifically referring to situations where this thinking:

1. Limits or blocks a person from being able to function in life and achieve their goals.
2. Causes extreme emotional reactions that lead a person to behaviors that harm themselves, others, or their opportunities in life.

3. Distorts reality, meaning that the thoughts are ignoring reality or facts in a way that is hindering a person's ability to make rational decisions or understand what is happening, in a way that has negative consequences.
4. Causes the person to judge and evaluate other people, themselves, or the world in a way that is harmful

As you can see, irrational thoughts are self-defeating and negatively impact our lives. If we do not learn how to identify and challenge our irrational thinking, we will continue to judge ourselves and others, remain blind to truths that could change our lives, experience emotional disturbances that harm us, and hold ourselves back from living our potential.

R = Rational: Irrational vs Rational Beliefs

The #1 goal of REBT is to change irrational beliefs into rational ones. Once the core limiting beliefs that are holding some back are disputed they can be replaced with new empowering ones. Other processes can be used to conquer irrational thoughts or emotional reactions at the surface, however dealing with the root of the problem—the underlying beliefs—is what makes lasting change possible. So, let's explore how to identify irrational beliefs and compare them to rational versions of the same beliefs.

Rational Belief	Irrational Belief
A rational belief is flexible For example: *"I want my co-worker to like me, but she does not have to like me"* This belief acknowledges what you want, which is for your co-worker to like you, but it is flexible because it also recognizes that you do not have to get what you want. It is not an absolute requirement or demand.	**An irrational belief is rigid** For example: *"My co-worker has to like me"* This belief doesn't just state what you want, it implies that it must be the case. You demand it. Because there is no flexibility, if she does not like you, you have no way of handling it.
A rational belief is non-extreme For example: *"It is bad if my co-worker doesn't like me, but it's not the end of the world"* This belief acknowledges that you find the situation negative, you think it's bad, but it also recognizes that it could be worse.	**An irrational belief is extreme** For example: *"It is the end of the world if my co-worker doesn't like me"* This belief is extreme because it expresses that you believe it could not be worse, when obviously it could be.

A rational belief is true	An irrational belief is false
Using the previous example: "*I want my co-worker to like me, but she does not have to like me*". Notice that this belief is made up of two parts: • "*I want my co-worker to like me....*" • "*.... but she does not have to like me*" Part 1: Is it true? Can you prove it? Well, since it's your own desire, yes, you can confirm this. It's true. Part 2: Is it true? You can logically prove that the other person does not have to like you because otherwise you would be denying them free will. Both parts are true, therefore the belief is true.	Using the previous example: "*My co-worker has to like me*". Again, this belief is made up of two parts: • "*I want my co-worker to like me....*" • "*.... and therefore she must like me*" Part 1: Is it true? Can you prove it? Again, this is your own desire, so yes. Part 2: Is it true? You cannot prove in any way that your co-worker has to like you. She has freewill and therefore this cannot be true. It is false. Because both parts are not true, this belief is false.
A rational belief is sensible	**An irrational belief is not sensible**
Does the belief "*I want my co-worker to like me, but she does not have to like me*" make sense? It does make sense because it's explicitly acknowledging that while you may want something that does not mean you have to get it.	Does the belief "*My co-worker has to like me*" make sense? No, it does not make sense because it asserts that wanting something means you have to have it. The two are not connected.
A rational belief is largely constructive	**An irrational belief is largely unconstructive**
When beliefs are rational they are usually constructive, meaning they lead to beneficial consequences. For example, if you believe: "*I want my co-worker to like me, but she does not have to like me*" and then your co-worker snaps at you for no good reason, this belief will lead you to the following consequences: • Emotional consequence: you'll be concerned about her response but not anxious about it • Behavioural consequence: If you address the situation with her, you will approach it in a reasonable way. • Thinking consequence: While you may suspect that she may be upset with you, you will recognize it is likely she is upset with someone or something else and it has nothing to do with you.	When beliefs are irrational they are usually destructive, meaning they lead to negative consequences . For example, if you believe: "*My co-worker must like me*" and your co-worker snaps at you for no good reason, this belief will lead you to the following consequences: • Emotional consequence: Her behaviour will make you anxious. • Behavioural consequence: You are likely to either avoid her or try desperately to get her to like you. • Thinking consequence: You will be certain that she is upset with you, rather than considering that there may be another reason for her behavior.

E = Emotive: Unhealthy vs Healthy Negative Emotions

It's common to hear people talk about negative and positive emotions. What most people are referring to is the fact that some emotions, such as happiness and excitement, are pleasant and others, like anger and sadness, are unpleasant. The problem arises when these different emotions are labeled good and bad. While happiness may feel good and sadness may feel bad, no emotions are entirely good or bad. If a psychopathic killer feels happy when they murder someone, would you say this is good? And if a person feels angry at themselves when they realize they did not take an opportunity they had been offered, and so they learn a lesson that will help them say yes to the next opportunity, is this bad?

Negative emotions may be unpleasant, but they are not bad, and labeling them that way will cause us to:

- Avoid situations that would elicit them
- Repress them when they do occur
- Judge ourselves or others for experiencing them

So, because emotions are not good or bad, it is more helpful to look at emotions as either healthy or unhealthy.

An **unhealthy negative emotion** is one that leads to unconstructive or harmful behavior or actions.

A **healthy negative emotion** is one that leads to constructive behavior or actions.

The truth about negative emotions is that each one of them has a healthy version and an unhealthy version. For example, anxiety is unhealthy but concern is healthy. Let's take a look at them now.

Anxiety vs Concern

Anxiety is a negative experience and it is unhealthy because it leads to unconstructive behaviors, such as:

- Withdrawing from the threat
- Avoiding the threat
- Seeking reassurance even though there is no way to get it
- Seeking safety from the threat

Of course, this may be justified if there is true danger, but what most people's brains label as a threat are minor life situations, such as someone saying something to us that makes us feel bad, having to experience uncertainty, or trying something new.

Concern, on the other hand, is a negative experience, yet it is healthy.

Concern leads to constructive behaviors, such as:

- Seeking to understand the threat
- Confronting the threat
- Seeking reassurance when it is possible

…which is usually reassuring themselves that the concern is only in their imagination and the likelihood of a truly negative outcome is very small.

Depression vs Sadness

Depression is a negative emotion that is unhealthy because it leads to prolonged withdrawal from enjoyable activities and it disrupts a person's ability to function in every-day-life.

Sadness, on the other hand, may feel negative but it is healthy because it leads a person to engage with enjoyable activities again after a brief period of mourning, loss, or unhappiness.

Guilt vs Remorse

Guilt is a negative emotion that is unhealthy because it leads to self-judgment, self-labeling as "bad", and often self-punishment. Due to feeling sorry for harm one inflicted, one may beg for forgiveness.

Remorse, on the other hand, may still feel negative, but it is healthy because it leads to acknowledgement of mistakes and taking responsibility for actions. Due to true empathy for the pain experienced by the other party, one may apologize and ask, but not beg for, forgiveness.

Shame vs Disappointment

Shame is a negative emotion that is unhealthy because it leads to withdrawal from others, avoiding eye contact, self-judgment, and self-punishment.

Disappointment, on the other hand, is a negative emotion that is healthy because it leads to keeping connection with others, maintaining eye contact, and acknowledging mistakes and taking responsibility for actions.

Hurt vs Sorrow

Hurt is a negative emotion that is unhealthy because it leads to sulking and withdrawal.

Sorrow is a negative emotion that is healthy because it leads to assertion and communicating with others.

Unhealthy Anger vs Healthy Anger

Unhealthy anger leads to aggression, both direct aggression and indirect or passive aggression.

Healthy anger leads to assertion and expression of concerns.

Unhealthy Jealousy vs Healthy Jealousy

Unhealthy jealousy leads to suspicion and prolonged questioning of the other party, checking in on them, and attempts at restricting them.

Healthy jealousy leads to reasonable, brief questioning of the other party and does not involve checking on or restricting the other them.

Unhealthy Envy vs Healthy Envy

Unhealthy envy leads to attempts to sabotage the other person's enjoyment of the desired possession or unhealthy feelings of anger or resentment toward the other party.

Healthy envy leads to striving to attain the desired possession for oneself, assuming it is truly desired, without any unhealthy feelings toward the other party.

B = Behavior: Unconstructive vs Constructive Behavior

In REBT behavior is defined as the actual action that is being taken by an individual, not just the thought. Irrational beliefs are what lead a person to irrational behaviors. When a behavior is irrational it is not constructive—it is harmful and leads to negative consequences. By developing rational beliefs, behaviors become constructive.

The reason this is so important is because there will always be situations in life that we could call adversity. The beliefs a person holds and the thoughts that they have about the situation will determine not only their emotional experience of it, but the behaviors they take and the resulting outcomes. Since adversity is inevitable, it is important to develop rational beliefs that help a person cope with adversity, choose constructive behaviors, and prevent unnecessary negative outcomes from situations that are already challenging.

So, put another way, when adversity happens and a person has irrational beliefs it leads to unconstructive behavior and when adversity happens and a person has rational beliefs it leads to constructive behavior.

If you want to change the behaviors, you need to change the belief.

Using the example we discussed in the Irrational vs Rational Beliefs section:

The adversity would be "My co-worker may not like me". The irrational belief would be "my co-worker must like me" and the unconstructive behavior would be avoiding of the co-worker or desperate attempts to get them to like me.

Looking at this same example but instead with a rational belief would look like this:

- The adversity would be "my co-worker may not like me".
- The rational belief would be "I want my co-worker like me, but she doesn't have to."
- The constructive behavior would be directly asking the co-worker if there is anything wrong.

There are two great examples of ways irrational beliefs lead to unconstructive behaviors.

1. **Short-term Self-protective Behavior:** Using our example, imagine the belief was more general and applied to all co-workers. Now the person believes "everyone I work with must like me." Since their driving force is to be liked they may develop a self-protective behavior that seems to benefit them in the short term but that is unconstructive in the long term. Because of this deep need to be liked, the person will be hypersensitive to everyone they work with. They will try to prevent others from not liking them by going out of their way to try to be liked. While the effort may work to make the person feel liked in the short term, the long-term unconstructive consequences would be preventing themselves from learning how the other people would treat them without being manipulated into appearing to like the person, as well as inauthentic relationships. Another possible long-term outcome would be causing the exact situation they fear by because even while smothering co-workers with kindness in attempt at being liked, the anxiety about being accepted would show through with behavior such as being guarded, defensive, or even avoiding social contact.

2. **Over-compensatory Behavior:** Another common unconstructive behavior that is triggered by irrational beliefs is the tendency to over-compensate for what the person fears. This means that the person is trying to prove themselves wrong about what they think is the truth about them, other people, or themselves. For example, if a person believes "I will not be able to deal with this obstacle", they will take on a greater obstacle in order to prove to themselves that they can, in fact, handle the original challenge or obstacle.

Another common example is workaholism. If a person believes "if I am not a high achiever I am defective, inferior, and will be rejected" they will work excessively in attempt at proving their status, success and self-worth. Unfortunately, because the underlying belief and fear is always there, no matter how much they achieve, they continue to feel the same way, which is shameful and unworthy.

Now, this doesn't mean that all workaholism is due to a need at proving a person's worth. Other times, overworking can be a coping strategy to avoid failure in another area. For example, a person who is struggling in their marriage may work excessively to avoid dealing with the failure of the marriage. They may hold an underlying irrational belief, such as "I cannot get divorced and if I do I am a failure and a bad person." This belief leads to the unconstructive behavior of over-working.

Another example is a person who is over-controlling of loved ones. The irrational belief they hold is that "people cannot be trusted" because they have experienced abuse, neglect, or extreme let down in their past. This belief leads to the behavior of being highly suspicious of others and actively manipulating or controlling them in attempt at preventing the possibility of being hurt.

The final example is a person who is rebellious. The irrational belief they hold is that "authority figures will dominate, bully, or control me." This belief leads to the behavior of rebelling against the desires and directives of authority figures in attempt at proving that they are autonomous and will not be controlled. They do this to avoid feeling hopeless or trapped.

Intellectual vs. Emotive Understanding

Even once you can identify that a belief is irrational, that the emotion is unhealthy, and that the resulting behavior is unconstructive, this doesn't necessarily mean you'll have the ability to change the emotion or the behavior to be constructive.

You see, there is a difference between understanding something at an intellectual level versus understanding it at an emotional level.

When a person is trying to transform an irrational belief into a rational one, it is important to recognize that simply understanding that the belief is rational is not enough to change it. For example, you may have a belief that your co-worker must like you. You may be able to rationalize with yourself and acknowledge that the belief is not rational. However, when your co-worker snaps at you, you still react emotionally by feeling anxious and you still behave based on the irrational belief by avoiding this co-worker.

We've all had experiences when we've known that our beliefs—such as our fears—make no sense logically, but we still feel afraid and act accordingly.

The only way to actually adopt the rational belief that your co-workers do not have to like you is to understand it at an emotional level. When you understand things at an emotive level you are also able to feel and behave differently. When you get to this point, thinking the new, rational, belief makes you feel better. It eases your anxiety. You may still feel negative emotions, such as concern, but you won't feel anxious or have a need to avoid your co-worker. You'll also easily transition at that point to other rational beliefs, such as "my co-worker may not be upset at me and may have other things bothering them."

Getting to the point of emotive understanding, when a new rational belief causes an emotional shift and changes behavior, can take time, repetition, and different processes. All of the REBT tools and strategies in the rest of this course are used to help develop this shift from intellectually understanding that our thinking is irrational to actually believing it and feeling the shift.

The Three Levels of Thinking

- REBT looks at three levels of thinking and they are:
- Inferences
- Evaluations
- Core Beliefs

Inferences

This level of thinking identifies "what is happening". Your mind processes what is happening around you and makes an assumption based on what you know, which may be limited, and whether it meets your expectations and demands. You then take your conclusion as a fact. This interpretation and perspective about reality all happens automatically and in a split second.

Evaluations

This level of thinking identifies "what does it mean?" Based on what your mind concludes about what is happening, it then evaluates the situation to determine what it means. It goes beyond simply the fact of reality, it assigns meaning to it. your needs and rules are met, it labels it good. If they're unmet, it labels it bad. And, depending on this final judgment, we will feel good or bad.

Core Beliefs

This level of thinking identifies "how life should be" and it exists at the unconscious level. In fact, all 3 levels of thinking are usually unconscious, however the beliefs or rules are the deepest level, meaning we're totally unaware we hold these beliefs. In REBT we look at the interference and evaluations, which are easier to identify, in order to figure out the core beliefs that drive the assumptions and judgments. The beliefs we hold about how life should be can be thought of as musts or demands. They are the rules we've developed for ourselves that tell us how we NEED things to be in life. One example could be that we believe we need to be approved of by others in order to be worthy.

The evaluation level of thinking is where our power lies to create change. Normally, this assigning of meaning and the resulting emotional response, again, happens automatically and unconsciously. However, by becoming aware of our emotional reactions or disturbances, as well as knowing the faulty way our minds tend to evaluate life situations so you can avoid them, we can choose constructive, rational ways of assigning meaning to events.

In the next section, we will dive deeper into understanding our human needs and beliefs, what types of beliefs lead to emotional disturbances, the dysfunctional ways we tend to assign meaning to situations, and the 3 core rules or musts that are the core of most of our irrational thinking and emotional pain.

And then in the rest of the course we'll dive into processes that will help make this entire process of thinking and interpreting our world CONSCIOUS, so we have more control over what we think and the emotions we experience because of it. We will learn how to develop awareness of emotional disturbances and questioning the meaning we assign them. We'll learn how to question our perception and assumptions and rewire the underlying beliefs that are the core of the problem.

The 6 Human Needs

At the core, our decisions and behaviors are driven by underlying needs and our beliefs about how these needs must be met. The 6 human needs are a powerful psychological framework, created by therapist Cloé Madanes and popularized by Anthony Robbins' strategic intervention strategies. These core needs are at the root of our motivations and why we prioritize certain decisions and actions, often without our awareness. Each person values one or more of these needs more than the others. Which need is your primary driver is a huge determining factor for how you live your life.

The 6 human needs are:
1. Certainty/comfort
2. Uncertainty/variety
3. Significance
4. Love and connection
5. Growth
6. Contribution

The first four needs are called the needs of the personality. These four needs are things that we always find ways to meet them—they are vital. The last two are called the needs of the spirit and are needs that are not always met. In most cases, the first four needs must be met before a person is able to start to value and focus on meeting the last 2 needs. However, when we meet those higher-level needs is when we truly feel fulfilled. Now let's look at each of them.

Need 1: Certainty/Comfort

At our core we want to feel that we are in control of our reality. This feeling gives us security. This allows us to feel comfortable in our life to feel that we can avoid pain and create pleasure. At the core this is just a survival mechanism that we have. Certainty makes us feel safe, emotionally, psychologically, and physically. Depending on how much we value certainty will depend how much risk we take in life. You probably have met people on both ends of the spectrum—those who want to control every single detail in their life and those that crave uncertainty. The extreme need for certainty, however, will hold you back because all growth and change requires uncertainty.

Need 2: Uncertainty/Variety

The second one is uncertainty. Yes, it's the opposite of the first one. Think about it—what would happen if you always knew everything that would happen to you? You would probably be bored to death. So, uncertainty brings excitement and spice to life. The level of uncertainty that you are willing and able to live with determines how much and how fast you will change. Keep in mind that being able to deal with uncertainty is also a skill that can be developed, as you become more confident that you can deal with change. Also, as you start associating uncertainty and change with something that creates happiness and helps you achieve your dreams, your desire for uncertainty will increase.

Need 3: Significance

Think about it, we all want to feel like we are special. We want to feel like we are important, needed and unique. There are a variety of ways that we can get significance. For example, you can get it by feeling like you are the best at something, by making a lot of money, having the best house in your neighborhood, by buying the latest thing, getting a master's degree or a doctorate, by becoming a social influencer, by being the best dad, having a bunch of tattoos, you can even be that person that has more problems that anyone else, the most intimidating, or even the most spiritual person. As you can see that there are endless ways to feel significant. People will go to great lengths to feel significant in their life.

Need 4: Love & Connection

The next need is Love and Connection. Whether we realize it or not, love is that thing that we need more than anything. When we love 100% we feel alive and it is a powerful force. For love, many people are willing to do extraordinary things for others, whether it's the love that a parent has for a child or the love of a romantic relationship. However, if we don't feel like we can get love, we settle for connection— even if these connections do not serve us. There are a lot of ways to get connection, whether it is through a friendship, a pet or even connecting to nature. Less-constructive ways of getting connection are through social media, sacrificing our authenticity to conform to a group, or people pleasing.

Need 5: Growth

The next one is the need for growth. Think about it if you're not growing in an area of your life, then that area is dying. This can be your relationship, your business, or an aspect of your personal life. If you are not growing than it does not matter what you are creating in your exterior world. That need for certainty can hold you back from growth, leading you to feel empty and not be able to feel true fulfillment. Growth can be scary because it can have uncertainty for some, but it brings fulfillment.

Need 6: Contribution

The last one is contribution and its one that many people reflect on in the later stages of life, as we look at our legacy. Contribution is like a higher level of the need for significance, the difference being that it's no longer about you. However, contribution is the essence of life. Life is not about me… it's about us. We are social creatures and we have a natural need to feel that we have a higher purpose and that our life has meaning. The way we find that is to contribute to others. In fact, the feeling that we are contributing to others can helps us overcome the biggest changes if we think it has a purpose. Life therefore is about creating meaning, and that comes from giving.

We each have a stronger need for some areas over others at different points in our lives. All of these beliefs are healthy, however we cause ourselves pain when we develop IRRATIONAL IDEAS about what we think we need in order to fulfill these core needs.

We need security, but we tell ourselves we need to be free of all discomfort and inconvenience at all times.

We need love, but we tell ourselves we need to be approved of by everyone at all times.

And, we develop emotional disturbances because of our irrational rules we create about meeting our needs.

So, which need a person values most, and which ones they are starving to meet, will influence the choices that they make in life. They will find a way to meet those needs one way or another, whether through a negative or positive way. For example, someone robbing someone can feel significant, have that thrill of uncertainty, and at the same time they feel certain because they are the one in control. So, this negative action can meet 3 core needs.

The power of identifying your own hierarchy of needs (which one/s are most important to you) is that you can then reflect to see if you're meeting your needs in constructive ways. (And, if not, consciously choose more constructive ways of meeting your needs.)

At the end of the day, fulfillment comes from something internal—whether, deep inside you feel loved, feel like you are growing, and contributing to others. This is why the higher level needs (further down the list) are what ultimately lead to fulfillment. However, in most cases, the lower level needs HAVE to be met in order for a person to turn their attention to the higher level needs.

Let's look at constructive ways of meeting these needs:

- **Certainty**: You can have certainty by having a daily routine or having a community around you that is supportive no matter what's happening in your life.
- **Variety**: You can have variety by adding diverse experiences to your life. You can also try new things and learn new skills.
- **Significance**: You can meet the need of significance by using your talents and skills. You can also master a skill and share your skills with others.
- **Love/Connection**: You can meet this need by establishing lifelong friendships spending more time with like-minded people, as well as improving your relationship skills.
- **Growth**: You can meet the need for growth by constantly learning. For example, reading new courses, watching YouTube videos, or following others that help you grow. You can also surround yourself with people that motivate you and challenge you to become a better person.
- **Contribution**: You can meet the need of contribution by sharing your talents and passions with others. You can also engage in causes that are meaningful to you.

So, ask yourself:

Which needs are the most important to you?

How do you currently meet these needs?

Which area of need are you currently struggling with the most?

In what way do you feel like your need is not being met?

What do you believe is necessary for your need to be met?

```



```

How can you meet these needs in a way that will help you truly be fulfilled?

```



```

Two Ways We Disturb Ourselves Emotionally

A disturbance is an unhealthy negative emotional reaction to a situation that is caused by an irrational belief. Our goal is to use REBT principles and processes to change the underlying beliefs that cause the disturbances. There are a number of different core beliefs that people can hold that will disturb themselves emotionally, but they fall into 2 general categories.

First, people can hold irrational beliefs about THEMSELVES, or what is often referred to as their ego. These beliefs often are also tied to beliefs about approval by others. This is called an Ego Disturbance.

Second, people can hold irrational beliefs about their emotional or physical COMFORT. This is called a Discomfort Disturbance. Most people tend to hold irrational beliefs in one of these categories more than the other.

1. Ego Disturbances are caused by placing unreasonable demands on ourselves, and when we don't meet those demands it impacts our self-image. For example, we may demand that we do well at something and that we must not fail, and we may also tie our need to do well to a need to be approved of by others. If we do not do well, we then feel shameful about our lack of competence and embarrassed due to the perceived scorn of disapproving others. The fear of not doing well and the resulting shame may lead us to avoid any situation in which we might fail or be disapproved of. This in turn may hold us back from what we want to do in life.

In what ways are you putting unreasonable demands on yourself?

```



```

How is this impacting your self-image, confidence, or life?

[ ]

2. Discomfort disturbances are caused by placing unreasonable demands on others and on outside situations. For example, we may believe that other people should treat us a certain way. We also may put demands on our environment and the circumstances that we live under. When these demands are unreasonable and our expectations are not met, we feel frustrated or uncomfortable. This disturbance causes harmful emotions and behaviors that would not exist, even in the same circumstances, if the irrational belief was not setting unreasonable expectations in the first place. Discomfort disturbances comes in two forms: low frustration tolerance and low discomfort tolerance. The two types are similar, and many times are associated or referred to as one and the same. Let's look at both more closely.

2.a. Low frustration tolerance happens when you demand that frustration must not happen in your life. This could be a belief that the world is supposed to make you happy or a belief that everything is supposed to be perfect or ideal. The problem occurs when life inevitably does not make you happy or isn't perfect because you will find the resulting frustration unbearable. You believe it shouldn't be happening. Instead of a minor frustration, it feels horrible.

You may also believe that things have to be the way that you want them to be. But then, when everything isn't exactly as you think it should be, you can't stand it and you make it more significant than it really is or needs to be. Your unrealistic expectation that everything is supposed to go your way makes it challenging to enjoy your world because you're always disappointed.

What have you been experiencing frustration about?

[ ]

What rule is this situation breaking?

[ ]

2.b. Low discomfort-tolerance on the other hand is when you believe that you should not experience emotional or physical discomfort or pain. Then when you experience any physical or emotional discomfort, you catastrophize it and make a big deal about it, like it's the end of the world. Then you don't just experience the pain or sadness, you find the experience absolutely intolerable! And so you are likely to avoid anything that may create any physical or emotional discomfort.

In what ways do you tend to experience emotional or physical discomfort?

On a scale of 1 to 10, how much does it bother you? ___

What do you tend to avoid in order to avoid discomfort?

There are a variety of ways that low discomfort-tolerance can negatively impact our lives. Which ones have you experienced?

- **Discomfort anxiety:** This is when we experience emotional tension when we feel that our comfort is threatened in any way.
- **Unnecessary worrying**: This is when we worry that the undesired situation may happen, and we dread it because we don't feel like we could stand it. We feel that we must worry about it just in case it happens.
- **Avoidance:** We may avoid experiences, events, or people that may create discomfort that we feel may be too hard to deal with or overcome.
- **Secondary disturbance:** This is when our disturbance creates a second disturbance. For example, we may feel anxious because we are worried that we may feel anxious. You can also be afraid of feeling fear. You can also feel angry at yourself for the behaviors that resulted from your anxiety. In each case you're adding another layer of negative emotion on top of the one you believe you should be experiencing.
- **Quick fix:** In order to cope with undesirable disturbances we may seek instant gratification or short-term pleasure, such as drugs or alcohol or even going on social media for a quick fix of approval.
- **Procrastination:** In this situation we put off doing something because we are avoiding a possible unpleasant situation or not wanting to deal with something that may be difficult or uncomfortable.
- **Negativity and complaining:** This is where we make a big deal about small setbacks, focus our attention on the negative aspects of a situation, ignoring the positive aspects, or compare the situation to other circumstances to highlight what's wrong with the situation, and then of course complain about it to others.

As you can, it's important to understand how our beliefs lead to emotional disturbances, aka undesirable, unhealthy stress, anxiety, anger and sadness. On top of our core beliefs we add another layer of disturbance when we judge situations and assign meaning. That's what we're going to talk about next. Then we'll look at the 3 core beliefs that cause the majority of people's emotional pain, all of which are based on demands we put on our self, others, and the world.

Evaluative Thinking: 4 Dysfunctional Ways We Assign Meaning

In the next sections we're going to look more closely at the 3 core beliefs that result from all irrational thinking. These beliefs are ultimately what cause our emotional disturbances. However, in order to develop an understanding of these beliefs and why they are problematic we need to look at the evaluative level of thinking. You'll recall that there are 3 levels of thinking: inference, which is when we decide what is going on, evaluation, which is when we decide what it means, and core beliefs, which are the underlying rules that dictate our inference and evaluation.

In REBT we look closely at the way that we evaluate what is going on around us because this is where we have the greatest power to change our thinking. You see, our beliefs are general and we don't put them to use until something happens and we can apply our rules to the situation and evaluate if they're being met. So, once individual situations happen in life, we evaluate what happens and decide what it means.

If you ask yourself or someone else "what does this mean" or "why does this matter" you'll easily get an answer. But if you immediately asked, "what is the belief that is causing you to have this emotion or think this way?" you would receive only a blank stare.

And, so, in the next section we will begin to look at the process for identifying irrational thinking and rooting out the underlying beliefs, and much of the work will be done at the evaluation level of thinking.

The reason it is so important to understand the way we tend to evaluate what happens in our lives is because the meaning we assign to situations is what ultimately causes our emotional and behavioral response to it. A situation may cause a result in our life at a practical level, but how we think and feel about it is what determines how we experience that result. We've mentioned the idea of a secondary disturbance before, which is when we experience a situation that is already unpleasant or challenging and we add another layer of disturbance by judging the situation in a way that upsets us. You can find yourself in a situation where you already feel upset because things aren't going your way and then you can make it worse by evaluating the situation and making a judgment that things are never going to go your way, which of course makes the experience worse.

There are 4 main destructive ways that we evaluate life circumstances, including: demanding, awfulizing, people-rating, and discomfort intolerance.

Demandingness:

The first one, demandingness, is actually the first step to evaluating what something means to us. The other evaluative processes build upon this one. Remember, when we talked about the rules or beliefs we create in attempt at meeting our needs, it isn't the core human needs that cause the problem, it is the demands we put on ourselves, others, and the world regarding what we belief is required for our needs to be met. It's reasonable to need love and belonging and to feel safe, but it's not reasonable to demand approval and unending comfort.

When a situation occurs, we evaluate it and ask ourselves "is this situation meeting my demands and expectations about myself, others, or the world?" Because the belief we hold tells us that these demands MUST be met, if the answer to the question is NO, it causes an emotional disturbance and leads to destructive behavior.

The two words to be on the lookout to spot a demanding belief or evaluation are the words "should" and "must".

In what areas of your life are you demanding that you or others "must" or "should" do something?

[ ]

The SOLUTION to demanding thinking is to turn the MUST into a PREFERENCE. Tell yourself, "I prefer it to be this way, but if it is not, that's okay too."

Awfulizing:

When a situation occurs, we evaluate it and ask ourselves "how bad is this?" And usually, because our demands aren't being met, our answer is that it's the worst-case scenario, it's horrible, it's awful. We may even ask ourselves "how likely is it to continue to happen or that there will be a terrible consequence?" And, of course, we're likely to think the answer is FOREVER and YES, and so we make it even worse. For example, if your boss tells you that he wants to meet with you, you may evaluate what it means and conclude that it must be something horrible—in fact, you're probably going to be fired. This will impact how you approach the meeting, your emotional state, your interactions with others and every other aspect of your life until you have that meeting. It may turn out that the meeting was to offer you a raise or promotion instead.

In what areas of your life are you awfulizing or making a big hairy deal about something that either isn't really a big deal or is a temporary problem?

[ ]

The SOLUTION to awfulizing is to remind yourself that it could be worse, it's not the end of the world, and it is temporary. Tell yourself "It's not the end of the world, this too shall pass."

People-rating:

When you or another person display a trait, behavior, or action that does not meet your demands, we evaluate them (or ourselves) and ask "what does this mean about them?" We look at the trait, behavior, or action and judge it as bad because it didn't meet our demand. But then we take it a step further and judge the person as bad too, as unworthy. We equate that one characteristic with the whole person, which ultimately puts ourselves and everyone we observe in a situation in which we have to be perfect in all areas in order to be deemed worthy. One flaw and we're judged as all bad.

This need to rate and judge ourselves leads to low self-confidence, defensiveness, and approval seeking behavior. In what ways do you tend to have low self-esteem? In what ways are you defensive? In what ways do you go out of your way to seek approval?

[ ]

The need to rate and judge others leads to feelings of superiority, mistreatment of others, and discrimination. In what ways do you tend to judge others, feel better than others, mistreat others, or discriminate against others?

```
┌─────────────────────────────────────────────────────────────────────┐
│                                                                       │
│                                                                       │
│                                                                       │
│                                                                       │
│                                                                       │
│                                                                       │
└─────────────────────────────────────────────────────────────────────┘
```

The SOLUTION to people-rating is to recognize that one trait or behavior does not define a person. Tell yourself "All people have both good and bad qualities and everyone is capable of changing and improving."

Discomfort intolerance:

We already talked at length about discomfort intolerance and the emotional disturbance caused by believing that one should never be uncomfortable and should always be perfect and approved of. When a situation occurs we evaluate it by asking "can I stand or tolerate this situation?" And because it doesn't meet our demands the answer is NO. The more uncomfortable it makes us, the more we will do whatever we can to avoid it, eliminate it, or avoid any other similar discomfort.

In what areas of your life do you tend to get really upset about being inconvenienced, disappointed, or frustrated?

```
┌─────────────────────────────────────────────────────────────────────┐
│                                                                       │
│                                                                       │
│                                                                       │
│                                                                       │
│                                                                       │
└─────────────────────────────────────────────────────────────────────┘
```

In what areas of your life do you tend to get really upset about physical discomfort or having unpleasant emotions?

```
┌─────────────────────────────────────────────────────────────────────┐
│                                                                       │
│                                                                       │
│                                                                       │
│                                                                       │
│                                                                       │
└─────────────────────────────────────────────────────────────────────┘
```

The SOLUTION to discomfort intolerance is to remember that perfection is impossible and that discomfort is a natural part of life. Tell yourself "I'm not perfect and neither is anyone else. We are all a work in progress. I might not like being uncomfortable, but sometimes the best things in life require stepping out of my comfort zone."

Major Must #1: APPROVAL—I must be approved of by others to be worthy.

Need: acceptance, belonging   **Fear:** judgment, rejection

Demands: I expect myself to perform well and win approval from all significant others at all times, and if not I am a failure, unworthy, and deserve to suffer.

Symptoms:

- Places unrealistic expectations on oneself
- Over-concern with what other people think
- Achievement and popularity determine self-worth
- Self-critical, lack of self-acceptance

Emotional Consequences

- Depression, feeling not good enough, unable to express or embrace true self
- Anxiety, worry about what others think, being judged
- Low confidence, feeling bad about yourself, others disapproval means we are bad

Behavioral Consequences

- Risk-avoidance, for fear of being judged for failing or being different
- Shyness, for fear of being embarrassed
- Procrastination, for fear of failure, judgment, risk
- Unassertiveness, for fear of rejection or criticism
- Workaholism, in order to gain approval

REPLACE WITH THIS RATIONAL BELIEF:

I have value as a human being simply by being my authentic self, and I desire love only from those who appreciate me and recognize the good in me.

False Sub-Belief: I need love and approval from EVERYBODY.

Consequence: Stifling of true self, lack of self-love and self-respect.

Truth:

- What matters most is self-acceptance, authenticity, and unconditional love from only the most significant others.
- Everyone has different tastes and preferences and it is impossible to be loved by everybody.
- By doing what others want or expect in order to gain approval, you are giving away your power to choose how you want to live your life.
- Trying too hard to be approved of has the opposite effect and others will not respect you.
- It may not be pleasant when other people do not like you, but the truth is that it isn't fatal and it doesn't really make a real difference in your life.

False Sub-Belief: I must be successful, intelligent and competent in all areas.

Consequence: Preoccupation with proving adequacy, even it if means looking competent when not.

Truth:

- It is totally natural to be better at some things than others. It is okay to not be good at something.
- You can improve any ability (including intelligence) if you put effort into improving.
- Being afraid of being bad at something can hold you back from trying new things that you're not already good at.
- Failure is a necessary part of growth and improvement.
- Focusing too much on being successful in order to impress others means you are taking time and energy away from things you may care more about.

False Sub-Belief: I must be dependent on other people because they are stronger than I am, and I can't depend on myself.

Consequence: Leads to unhealthy relationships that burden others and creates attachment based on need rather than genuine love. Doing only what you need help to do actually limits your potential because in most cases your need to depend on others actually holds you back from doing more.

Truth:

- It is true that we all need others to help us learn and to support us during challenging situations, however support from others is meant to be temporary and only as needed, with the goal of helping us get to a place where we are caring for ourselves.
- Many people are perfectly capable of doing things on their own but they continue to tell themselves they need others to help them because they are afraid to let go of control of the other person.
- The more you continue to allow others to do things for you the less skill you will develop and the lower your confidence will be.
- If you depend on others to feel safe and confident, there will inevitably be a time they cannot be there for you, which actually makes you less safe and confident than you would be if you relied on yourself.

False Sub-Belief: My past has made me who I am and will continue to define my future.

Consequence: Continuing to live patterns that do not serve you and failure to reach your potential due to unwillingness to take responsibility for your life.

Truth:

- When you were younger, you did not understand what was happening, and therefore it impacted your behavior automatically. However, now you have the ability to think about your past and present differently and choose to act differently.
- When you were a child, you had no control over what happened in your life, however as an adult you do have control over the decisions you make.
- The past is simply a memory in your mind and has absolutely no way of literally influencing your future. If you are continuing to experience situations that existed in your past that you do not want, you have the option to change them.
- It is true that your past experiences influenced your belief systems, behaviors, and situations you experience in your life today, but now that you know you have a choice all of those things can be changed going forward.

Major Must #2: JUDGMENT—Other people must do "the right thing" and meet my expectations in order to be worthy.

Need: importance, superiority   **Fear:** unfairness, disappointment

Demands: expect all significant others to treat me kindly and fairly, as well as act appropriately, and if they don't, they are unworthy, rotten people who deserve to be punished

Symptoms:

- Unrealistic expectations on others, including expecting them to be infallible, perfect
- Assuming you are the sole authority on what is right and wrong
- Assuming you have authority over others
- Believing everyone else is responsible for catering to your needs

Emotional Consequences

- Anger, rage or fury when others intentionally or unintentionally treat you poorly or unfairly or don't meet your expectations
- Impatience with others who make mistakes or aren't perfect
- Bitterness against others for not meeting your needs
- Resentment toward others for being imperfect and especially for treating you unfairly or not meeting your needs

Behavioral Consequences

- Aggression and violence as a way of punishing others for being inappropriate or not meeting expectations
- Bigotry and intolerance of anyone who does not meet your definition of right and wrong
- Bullying others to enforce your belief of the way others should behave or be
- Nagging others to elicit the right action you expect and require

REPLACE WITH THIS RATIONAL BELIEF:

All people, including myself, are imperfect, have value to offer, and have a unique perspective of the world.

False Sub-Belief: I should be concerned and upset about other people's problems.

Consequence: Wasted energy while focused on other people's problems rather than focusing on directing your own life.

Truth:

- Other people's problems almost never have anything to do with you.
- Getting upset because someone else is upset or has a problem does not help them feel better or fix their problem.
- Upsetting yourself about someone else' problem causes you to experience negative emotions for no good reason.

- You do not have the power to change other people or their problems, and reacting emotionally to their problem lessens your ability to support them if that is your goal.
- Focusing on other people's problems takes away time and energy from improving your own life.

False Sub-Belief: Everyone should treat each other, and especially me, in a fair, considerate manner or they should be punished.

Consequence: Harsh condemnation of and possible lashing out at anyone who does not treat you the way you want to be treated, which is your definition of fairness.

Truth:

- While it is nice to want everyone to act kindly and, specifically, behave in a way that pleases you, however you do not hold authority over other people and it is not your role to punish people for their behavior.
- Not everyone has the same definition of fairness or being considerate, and therefore they may act differently than you would expect, however this does not make them a bad person.
- Punishing someone for how they treat another person is not only not effective in changing their behavior, the person punishing them is often exhibiting a worse behavior than the original offense.

False Sub-Belief: People must be competent and act wisely and if not they have no value and should be punished.

Consequence: Shaming, criticizing, and rejecting others for mistakes, errors, or undeveloped abilities.

Truth:

- This hyper-judgment of others is what causes the cultural perpetuation of approval seeking behavior.
- Everyone naturally has different levels of ability in different areas, however all people are capable of growing in improving in all areas.
- Usually, a person's ability, or lack thereof, is more of a factor of their life circumstances than natural talent.
- When someone makes a mistake or a decision you deem "unwise" there is always a reason behind it, such as not knowing any better, doing the best they are able to do at the time, or having other influences causing their behavior.
- Even if a person has a low level of competence, they still have innate value and dignity as a human being and are worthy of respect.
- Even if a person makes poor choices it does not mean they are not capable of acting more intelligently in another situation where they have different access to information, options, and experience.

False Sub-Belief: When other people behave badly it means they are bad and should be punished.

Consequence: When others make mistakes or do things you disapprove of, judging them as bad and punishing them: a) equates the behavior with the person and b) does not lead to any form of improvement or resolution.

Truth:

- Human beings are not perfect and make mistakes.
- A person's behavior in one moment does not define their character or worthiness.
- Everyone has a reason for why they act the way they do.
- Everyone has a different perspective of what is right and wrong.
- Punishing someone for their actions does not address the underlying reason for their actions and therefore does not teach them anything.

Major Must #3: COMFORT—Life must be easy, without discomfort or inconvenience.

Need: certainty, comfort, justice   **Fear:** adversity, uncertainty, discomfort
Demands: expect all external conditions to be pleasant and favorable at all times and when they're not it is awful and unbearable.

Symptoms:

- Unrealistic expectations about life being perfect
- Belief that living a trouble-free life is a birthright
- Lack of belief in your ability cope with adversity
- Complete rejection of all life problems as unacceptable

Emotional Consequences

- Low frustration tolerance
- Self-pity and "poor me" attitude
- Depression, hopelessness
- Discomfort anxiety

Behavioral Consequences

- Procrastination
- Shirking
- Drug and alcohol abuse
- Overindulgence in "feel good" behaviors (e.g., overeating)

REPLACE WITH THIS RATIONAL BELIEF:

It is perfectly natural for life conditions to not be ideal or perfect and it's okay if situations do not exist the way I would prefer because I am capable of finding solutions to problems and making changes that bring me happiness and opportunity regardless of the situations that happen around me.

False Sub-Belief: Things must go the way I want them to go and I should have control over them.

Consequence: Anger and frustration when things don't go the way you want does not help you change the situation. Expecting everything to be exactly as you want it gives away your power to be happy until everything is perfect, which it won't be, ever.

Truth:

- In most situations outside conditions are almost completely outside of your control.
- It is perfectly natural and inevitable for life situations to be unpredictable, uncertain, and rarely to happen the way you believe they should.
- What you do have control over is what happens internally, such as your thoughts and emotions about a situation.
- It is not the outside world and it's conditions that will make you happy and satisfied with life, it is your internal dialog and the perspective you choose to take of those situations.

- It isn't the bad situations that make you unhappy, it's the belief that they shouldn't happen that make you unhappy.
- When something you don't like happens, you can either change it or you can't. If you can change it, take action. If you can't change it, identify what is or could be good about it, how you could get around it, or what you can learn.

False Sub-Belief: If something is or may be dangerous or unpleasant I should continue to worry about it.

Consequence: Unnecessary worry causes anxiety and stress and takes away time and energy from productive solutions or other important aspects of life

Truth:

- Worrying about something does not, under any circumstance, impact the outcome.
- It is normal to feel concerned or anxious about a potential problem, however catastrophizing about it and telling yourself how awful it will be and continuing to obsess over it is completely unnecessary.
- If potential danger or problems can be dealt with ahead of time, take responsibility to identify when and if action can be taken.
- If nothing can be done about the situation, there is no benefit to upset yourself by continuously thinking about it. Worrying does not prevent it from happening. If it's going to happen anyway, you benefit more from being in a more calm, healthy emotional place between now and then.
- In many cases, worrying about something that may happen can actually increase the likelihood of it happening. For instance, if you are driving and you are worried about getting in a car accident, this will make you nervous and your driving abilities will be impaired, making you more likely for you to make a mistake and cause an accident.

False Sub-Belief: My unhappiness, sorrow, and disturbance are caused by unpleasant or undesirable situations, and therefore I must avoid these situations.

Consequence: Preoccupation with controlling situations and people, leading to frustration when faced with the fact that this is not possible. Avoidance of anything that could go wrong, which leads to a very limited life.

Truth:

- Your unhappiness and disturbance is caused by judgment of the undesirable situations, not by the situations themselves.
- You have the ability to choose different ways of thinking about other people or situations that makes you feel better.
- It is okay to feel bad about situations and telling yourself the situations should not be there and that you should not feel bad only ads another layer of feeling bad on top of it.

False Sub-Belief: It is easier to avoid, rather than face and deal with, life's difficulties, challenges and responsibilities.

Consequence: By avoiding difficulties you avoid the potential positive benefit of facing them, plus in many cases you are only putting off problems that you will need to face later, when they will often be worse.

Truth:

- Putting off responsibilities, such as procrastinating, only makes the task harder and more stressful.
- Almost all worthwhile pursuits, accomplishments, goals, and experiences require some level of challenge or unpleasant activity. Therefore, avoiding difficulty prevents you from ever experiencing the desired outcome.
- The more we do something, the less difficult it becomes. In order to get better at anything we first have to experience it being challenging.
- If we do only what is easy we live a very boring experience, limited only to what we are already comfortable with.
- It is perfectly natural and okay to struggle with challenges and responsibilities and it's okay to feel uncomfortable while you overcome them and improve your abilities.

False Sub-Belief: I am supposed to just be happy. I do not have control over my emotions.

Consequence: When you are not happy all the time you will either blame yourself for being unworthy or blame the outside for not meeting your expectations and making you happy.

Truth:

- While happiness can spontaneously arise when pleasant situations exist in your life, happiness does not depend on favorable external conditions.
- While it is perfectly normal and natural to have an automatic emotional response to situations in life, it is not the situation itself that causes the emotion, it is the result of the way you think about and judge the stations that happened.
- Happiness can be experienced even simply at the thought of something pleasant, just like anger can be experienced simply by imagining being mistreated. In both cases, the situation is not actually happening, however the emotion is just as real.
- Therefore, emotions are caused by your thoughts, not by situations.
- Happiness is a choice, and long-term, lasting happiness has been proven to be the result of making choices to a) choose a positive perspective of life situations and b) make choices to live in ways that allow you to express your creativity and passions, as well as contributing to others.

False Sub-Belief: All problems must have a perfect solution and that solution must be found.

Consequence: Inability to accept the reality of a situation and take action to make improvements because the solution is not perfect. Obsession with making a situation perfect, which often makes it worse.

Truth:

- There is almost never a solution to a problem that leads to a perfect outcome.
- Expecting a solution to be perfect will prevent you from identifying possible options or moving forward with any solution at all.

Use the Core Belief Identification Chart on the following pages to identify what type of belief is at the root of your current problem and refer to the ABCDEF process in the following section.

Core Beliefs Identification Chart

3 Levels of Beliefs

Which category does your belief fall under? Which question are you asking yourself?

INFERENCE *(Interpretation or Perspective)* **Asking "What is happening?"**	EVALUATION *(Demanding, Awfulizing, People-Rating, Discomfort Intolerance)* **Asking "What does it mean?"**	CORE BELIEFS *(Approval, Judgment, Comfort)* **Asking "How do you believe life should be?"**
What are you assuming? What information might you be missing?	Who are you evaluating? You, someone else, the world? What is your conclusion or judgment?	Who or what is not following your rules or living up to your expectations?
See ABCDEF Step 3 (D) PERSPECTIVE	*See ABCDEF Step 4 (D) MEANING*	*See ABCDEF Step 5 (D) BELIEFS*

Identifying Core Beliefs

Step 1: Identify the problem you are having—the activating event, emotional disturbance, or undesirable consequences?

My Problem (Event, Disturbance, Etc.):

Step 2: Go through the following 3 checklists and check off each situation you are experiencing related to this specific problem. Then, tally up your check marks to see which core belief is at the root of your problem.

CORE BELIEF #1—APPROVAL I must be approved of by others to be worthy.
SITUATIONS/EXPERIENCES
Places unrealistic expectations on oneself
Over-concern with what other people think
Achievement and popularity determine self-worth
Self-critical, lack of self-acceptance
Depression, feeling not good enough, unable to express or embrace true self
Anxiety, worry about what others think, being judged
Low confidence, feeling bad about yourself, others disapproval means we are bad, can't be yourself
Risk-avoidance, for fear of being judged for failing or being different
Shyness, for fear of being embarrassed
Procrastination, for fear of failure, judgment, risk
Unassertiveness, for fear of rejection or criticism
Workaholism, in order to gain approval

Total: _____ of 12

On a scale of 1 to 10, how much does the following belief relate to your problem? I expect myself to perform well and win approval from all significant others at all times, and if not I am a failure, unworthy, and deserve to suffer.

1 --10

Which of the following sub-beliefs most closely relates to your problem?
1. I need love and approval from EVERYONE.
2. I must be successful, intelligent, and competent in all areas.
3. I must be dependent on other people because they are stronger than I am, and I can't depend on myself.
4. My past has made me who I am and will continue to define my future.

How would you re-word the sub-belief you selected so it captures the belief that is leading to your problem?

CORE BELIEF #2—JUDGMENT
Other people must do "the right thing" and meet my expectations in order to be worthy.
SITUATIONS/EXPERIENCES
Places unrealistic expectations on others, expecting them to be infallible/perfect
Assuming you are the sole authority on what is right and wrong
Assuming you have authority over others
Believing others are responsible for catering to your needs
Anger, rage, or fury when others, intentionally or unintentionally, treat you poorly or unfairly or don't meet your expectations
Impatience with others who make mistakes or aren't perfect
Bitterness against others for not meeting your needs
Resentment toward others for being imperfect and especially for treating you unfairly or not meeting your needs
Aggression and/or violence as a way of punishing others for being inappropriate or not meeting expectations
Bigotry and intolerance of anyone who does not meet your definition of right and wrong
Bullying others to enforce your belief of the way others should behave or be
Nagging others to elicit the right action you expect and require

Total: _____ of 12

On a scale of 1 to 10, how much does the following belief relate to your problem? I expect all significant others to treat me kindly and fairly, as well as act appropriately, and if they don't, they are unworthy, rotten people who deserve to be punished

1 --10

Which of the following sub-beliefs most closely relates to your problem?

1. I should be concerned and upset about other people's problems.
2. Everyone should treat each other, and especially me, in a fair, considerate manner or they should be punished.
3. People must be competent and act wisely and if not they have no value and should be punished.
4. When other people behave badly it means they are bad and should be punished.

How would you re-word the sub-belief so it captures the belief that is leading to your problem?

CORE BELIEF #3—COMFORT
Life must be easy, without discomfort or inconvenience.
SITUATIONS/EXPERIENCES
Having unrealistic expectations about life being perfect
Belief that living a trouble-free life is a birthright
Lack of belief in your ability to cope with adversity
Complete rejection of all life problems as unacceptable
Low frustration tolerance
Self-pity and "poor me" attitude
Depression, hopelessness
Discomfort anxiety
Procrastination
Shirking responsibility
Drug and alcohol abuse
Overindulgence in "feel good" behaviors (e.g. overeating)

Total: _____ of 12

On a scale of 1 to 10, how much does the following belief relate to your problem? I expect all external conditions to be pleasant and favorable at all times and when they're not it is awful and unbearable.

1 ---10

Which of the following sub-beliefs most closely relates to your problem?
1. Things must go the way I want them to go and I should have control over them.
2. If something is or may be dangerous or unpleasant I should continue to worry about it.
3. My unhappiness, sorrow, and disturbance are caused by unpleasant or undesirable situations, and therefore I must avoid these situations.
4. It is easier to avoid, rather than face and deal with, life's difficulties, challenges and responsibilities.
5. I am supposed to just be happy. I do not have control over my emotions.
6. All problems must have a perfect solution and that solution must be found.

How would you re-word the sub-belief you selected so it captures the belief that is leading to your problem?

```



```

Step 3: Review the "truth" statements that correspond to the sub-belief. You can find these earlier in this section. Then, ask yourself the following questions:

Which of the "truth" statements do I find the most believable and empowering?

```



```

How would I re-word any of them to turn them into affirmations I could repeat to myself to re-train my thinking in this area?

```



```

Step 4 Below are examples of *rational* versions of the 3 Core Irrational Beliefs:

- Belief 1: "I expect myself to perform well and win approval from all significant others at all times, and if not I am a failure, unworthy, and deserve to suffer" could be replaced with, "I have value as a human being simply by being my authentic self, and I desire love only from those who appreciate me and recognize the good in me."
- Belief 2: "I expect all significant others to treat me kindly and fairly, as well as act appropriately, and if they don't, they are unworthy, rotten people who deserve to be punished" could be replaced with, "All people, including myself, are imperfect, have value to offer, and have a unique perspective of the world."
- Belief 3: "I expect all external conditions to be pleasant and favorable at all times and when they're not it is awful and unbearable" could be replaced with, "It is perfectly natural for life conditions to not be ideal or perfect and it's okay if situations do not exist the way I would prefer because I am capable of finding solutions to problems and making changes that bring me happiness and opportunity regardless of the situations that happen around me."

Write a NEW, rational, empowering belief that you wish to replace the irrational belief.

```



```

The ABCDEF Journaling Process for Changing Irrational Beliefs

All of the different elements of irrational thinking and beliefs that we've learned about can be summed up in one belief: "I am supposed to always get what I want and feel the way I want, and other people and the world must meet these demands."

Deep down what we're really trying to do is keep ourselves safe, be loved, and feel good about ourselves. The underlying drive behind all of this is natural and healthy—but because sometimes our needs aren't met and we don't feel safe or loved or good about ourselves our brains have to try to explain why. We believe that even just the thought that we might not get what we want is cause for concern. The first thing our brain tries to do is to control everything in life. This is where our demanding beliefs come from. The brain believes that if we establish an absolute rule that our needs will be met, we can force life into submission.

But of course, it doesn't work. When these demands are not met, our brain needs to explain WHY the rules were broken and our needs weren't met. Unfortunately, instead of recognizing that the core belief that everything is supposed to be perfect and under our control is WRONG, it develops new beliefs to explain the problem. These beliefs are usually one of these three things:

1. I am bad or unworthy.
2. They are bad or unworthy.
3. This is the end of the world and I am a victim.

The main premise is that both the underlying rule and the judgment we make when it isn't met are UNTRUE and our demands are NEVER going to be met, and therefore this is the cause of our emotional disturbances.

So, if we can identify and change the core beliefs, we can turn our negative, unhealthy emotional disturbances into healthy emotional reactions that lead to constructive behaviors and desired outcomes. Instead of feeling like other people and the world are blocking us from reaching our goals, we can develop a belief system that helps us stop ourselves from using life circumstances as an excuse to sabotage our own success. So, how do we do this?

Step 1) First, we identify the PROBLEM by becoming aware of the dysfunctional thinking that's going on.

This has 3 steps:
A. Which stands for **ACTIVATING EVENT**: Something happens.
B. Which stands for **BELIEF**: You hold a belief about the situation.
C. Which stands for **CONSEQUENCE**: You have an emotional reaction and a behavioral reaction, which also lead to consequences in our lives.

It is very important to notice that the entire point that REBT is trying to make is that A does not cause C directly. A situation that happens in life is not what causes us to feel or act a certain way. It is our BELIEF about the situation that causes how we feel and act. However, often it is not obvious what belief is influencing the emotional and behavioral consequences. When working through this process, recognize that often you will need to reflect on the activating event and the emotional and behavioral consequences FIRST in order to then figure out the belief beneath them.

For example:
A. **Activating Event**: Your employer accuses you of taking money from the register when you didn't.
B. **Belief**: You believe, "She has no right to do that. She is looking for a reason to fire me!"

C. **Consequences**: You feel angry and take action based on how you feel, which may be to lash out, putting your job in jeopardy.

In this situation, the lashing out would be a sign that there is a rule being broken, meaning an irrational belief is leading to the unconstructive behavior.

If your belief about the situation was different, your emotional response would have been different:

A. Your employer accuses you of taking money from the register (even though you didn't).

B. You believe, "I can't lose my job!."

C. You feel anxious and take action based on how you feel, which may be shutting down and being unable to bring up your feelings with your boss.

This belief leads to a different outcome, but it is still actually an irrational belief. It may be true that you don't want to lose your job, but focusing on how terrible it would be causes anxiety which gets in the way of a successful outcome. A rational belief would be to believe "I understand that someone took money from the register and that my boss believes it was me. It is hurtful to think she believes I would do that, but it's just a misunderstanding. I can talk to her about the situation and help her understand that it was not me. I don't want to lose my job, so I want to approach this with care." Of course, you would still feel a little angry, offended, and concerned, but you wouldn't be lashing out or shutting down. You'd be experiencing healthy negative emotions and dealing with the situation with constructive behaviors.

So, the goal of the first step is to identify what is going on and then identify the problem, which is the irrational belief. The reason the belief is the problem is because it is what leads to the undesirable emotions and behaviors that lead to the undesirable negative consequence.

Step 2) Next, we dispute the irrational beliefs—this is step D.

D—Disputing Irrational Thinking. This step includes all 3 levels of irrational thinking.

1. The first part is addressing our inferences or assumptions. Even though when identifying the irrational thinking we said that our inferences were part of the activating event itself, in order to change these assumptions we need to address them separately, which we do at this step in which we're disputing irrational beliefs.

2. The second part is addressing our evaluations and how we assign meaning. While REBT focuses primarily on this part, you will be learning processes for addressing all 3 levels of thinking throughout this course.

3. The third part is addressing the underlying beliefs and changing them to into rational beliefs. This is the ultimate goal of using REBT.

Step 3) Lastly, we create strategies for change.

Now that we have questioned the irrational beliefs and identified the desired rational beliefs, we have two additional steps to take:

Step E—Identify the New Effect we want to experience, which is really identifying the desired consequences, including how we want to feel, behave, and the result we want to experience.

Step F—Identify Further Action that is needed in order to avoid repeating the same irrational thinking or behavior and create lasting change.

So, we have ABCDEF Activating Event, Beliefs, Consequences, Disputing, New Effect, and Further Action. In the next sections we will explore each step in greater detail, and then in the next sections we will explore processes for changing beliefs by becoming aware of the problem areas, disputing irrational beliefs, and creating strategies for change.

Simplified ABCDEF Journaling Form

In the next sections you will learn more about this process, however return here for an easy to use, summarized method for walking through this journaling process. You are also welcome to use a journal to work through this process, or visit the website for this course to download a printable version of this form, as well as other worksheets for other material in this course.

A = Activating Event > What's going on?

What is the situation or problem?
- Is it: real   imagined
- Is it: past   present   future
- Is it: external (happening outside of you)   internal (happening inside of you)
- Is it: event   experience   person   emotion   thought   behavior   other

Describe the activating event:

What are you experiencing?

Emotions/Feelings?   How intense (1 to 10)?

Physical sensations?   How intense (1 to 10)?

If these emotions or sensations happened in the past, during the experience, what are you feeling NOW?   How intense (1 to 10)?

What are you thinking?

What automatic thoughts did you about the event while it was happening?

[blank text box]

What did you infer or how did you interpret what was happening?

[blank text box]

What did you assume?

[blank text box]

How much did you believe these thoughts and assumptions while you thought them (1 to 10)? ____

B = Beliefs > What are your rules?

What are your evaluative beliefs or judgments?

What does this mean?

[blank text box]

Why is this happening?

[blank text box]

Does it meet my expectations or rules? Which rules does it break?

[blank text box]

What is wrong about this situation? Why is this wrong?

How do you feel about the fact that this is happening?

What does it say about you or the people involved?

What TYPE of evaluative beliefs are these?

- Demands (musts and shoulds)
- Awfulizing (catastrophic)
- Discomfort/Frustration Intolerance
- People-rating (of self or others)

What are your core irrational beliefs?

Which of my rules for how life is supposed to be are being broken?

Rules about myself and being approved of by others?

Rules about how other people must behave in order to be worthy?

[ ]

Rules about how live is supposed to be—meaning if it's meeting my demands for living without discomfort, frustration, or inconvenience.

C = Consequences > What is your response and what is the resulting outcome?

What unhealthy negative emotions are you experiencing?

What are the major unhealthy negative emotions that you are experiencing about this event? (Unhealthy negative emotions: anxiety, depression, guilt, shame, rage, hurt, jealousy, envy)

[ ]

How did you feel DURING the event?

[ ]

What thoughts were you thinking that lead to this feeling?

[ ]

How do you feel now ABOUT this event?

[ ]

What thoughts are you thinking now that lead you to feel this way?

How do you feel about the future consequences of this event?

What thoughts do you have about how this will impact your future?

What self-defeating or unconstructive behaviors have you done?

How did you react to the situation? What did you say? Do? Think?

How have you responded to the situation since it happened up until now? How have you behaved? What did you say or do?

- Have you used any self-protective or over-compensatory behaviors, such as:
  - Going out of your way to please people
  - Overcompensating to make up for something
  - Pushing yourself too hard
  - Avoiding potentially challenging, uncertain, or unpleasant situations
  - Working too hard or trying to prove your worthiness
  - Trying too hard to control other people or situations
  - Being rebellious in attempt at proving your autonomy
  - Other:

```
┌─────────────────────────────────────────────────────────────────────┐
│                                                                       │
│                                                                       │
│                                                                       │
│                                                                       │
│                                                                       │
│                                                                       │
└─────────────────────────────────────────────────────────────────────┘
```

What have been the results, outcomes, or repercussions that have happened because of these emotions and behaviors?

How has how you felt or feel about the situation impacted you? Others (who, specifically)?

```
┌─────────────────────────────────────────────────────────────────────┐
│                                                                       │
│                                                                       │
│                                                                       │
│                                                                       │
│                                                                       │
│                                                                       │
└─────────────────────────────────────────────────────────────────────┘
```

What has happened because of how you felt?

```
┌─────────────────────────────────────────────────────────────────────┐
│                                                                       │
│                                                                       │
│                                                                       │
│                                                                       │
│                                                                       │
└─────────────────────────────────────────────────────────────────────┘
```

Can you see how your emotions influenced your behaviors and actions? Which emotions are connected to which behaviors?

```
┌─────────────────────────────────────────────────────────────────────┐
│                                                                       │
│                                                                       │
│                                                                       │
│                                                                       │
│                                                                       │
└─────────────────────────────────────────────────────────────────────┘
```

What have been the results or outcomes that occurred because of your actions or behaviors? Which behaviors have resulted in which outcomes?

```
┌─────────────────────────────────────────────────────────────────────┐
│                                                                       │
│                                                                       │
│                                                                       │
│                                                                       │
│                                                                       │
└─────────────────────────────────────────────────────────────────────┘
```

What future consequences do you anticipate will happen if you continue with these emotions, actions and behaviors?

What will happen because of these outcomes?

```
┌─────────────────────────────────────────────────────────────────────┐
│                                                                       │
│                                                                       │
│                                                                       │
│                                                                       │
│                                                                       │
└─────────────────────────────────────────────────────────────────────┘
```

Have you had any secondary emotional disturbances?

Looking back at how you felt and acted during the situation, how do you feel ABOUT it?

Looking at how you have behaved or felt SINCE the experience, or now, how do you feel ABOUT it?

How do you feel about the results or outcomes that have arisen because of how you felt and acted?

Imagining the future consequences that you anticipate will result from continuing these thoughts, emotions, and actions, how do you feel ABOUT the future?

D = Disputing > In what ways is your thinking irrational?

Refer to the inferences you identified in step A, specifically the thoughts and assumptions you had about the activating event. Review each inference separately.

Are they true? How do you know?

What are you assuming?

[ ]

Could you be wrong?

[ ]

How else could you interpret this situation?

[ ]

What is an alternative way you could think about this? Or, what could you say differently to yourself?

[ ]

How much do you believe this new way of thinking?

[ ]

Refer to the evaluations and judgments you identified in B.

What are you demanding?

Must it absolutely happen that way or is it possible that it would not?

[ ]

What would happen if you didn't get what you wanted?

What would this look like if you simply preferred it instead of demanded it?

How would you feel about it?

Are you awfulizing or catastrophizing anything?

How terrible did/does it feel on a scale of 1 to 10? ___

If it feels like the worst case scenario, could it actually be worse?

In comparison to other things that are worse, is this really THAT horrible?

Now that you think about it, how would you ACTUALLY rate how bad this is on a scale of 1 to 10? ___

Are you avoiding discomfort or frustration because you feel like it's intolerable?

How terrible did you initially feel like this inconvenience or irritation would be?

Would it actually be that bad? Would you survive? Is it the end of the world?

Is it possible that not facing the discomfort or frustration could actually make things WORSE?

What would be the negative consequences of continuing to avoid it?

Are you people-rating yourself or others?

Is it possible that the other person (or you) has a reasonable explanation for their behavior? What could it be?

If the person (or you) made a mistake, is it possible that they will do better next time?

If the person (or you) is insufficient in a certain area, does this mean they are insufficient in all areas?

```



```

If the person (or you) is flawed in one way, does it mean they are defective or unworthy overall?

```



```

If a person (or you) behaves in a way you believe is undesirable or bad, does it automatically mean they are a bad person?

```



```

How would it benefit you and the other party if you accepted that all people are imperfect, yet capable of improvement?

```



```

Refer to the musts and core beliefs you identified in B. Again, refer to the Core Belief Identification Chart if needed.

Which of the 3 major musts applies to your irrational beliefs?
 Approval   Judgment   Comfort

```



```

Ask yourself the following questions for EACH of the irrational core beliefs you've identified:

```



```

What is the irrational core belief?

[empty text box]

Why do you believe it? Why does this matter? (For example, you would ask yourself: why must I always get everything right? Why must everyone approve of me? Why does everyone have to love me?)

[empty text box]

What is irrational or illogical about it?

[empty text box]

What evidence can you think of that proves this belief wrong?

[empty text box]

How could you re-write the belief so that it would be based on TRUTH and be rational?

[empty text box]

E = New Effect > What is your preferred reaction and desired outcome?

How would you like to experience the ACTIVATING EVENT if it were to happen again?
Do you expect to be faced with a similar situation again in the future?

[empty text box]

How would you prefer to feel (what are the healthy negative emotions you could shift to)?

How would you like to interpret the situation next time? How is this different from the first time?

How would you have to think differently in order to feel the way you want to?

How would making these changes impact you?

How would you like to change your EVALUATIVE BELIEFS and assign meaning differently?

How would you prefer to evaluate this situation?

What would you like to believe that this means?

What would you need to think or do differently to make this change?

[ ]

How would making these changes impact you?

[ ]

What would you like to believe that is rational that replaces your IRRATIONAL CORE BELIEFS?

Which specific beliefs are at the core of what's going on here?

[ ]

How could you change each of these specific beliefs to be more rational?

[ ]

What do you want to believe?

[ ]

How would making these changes impact you?

[ ]

What were or are the emotional consequences of your beliefs?

How would you prefer to feel about the situation?

```
[                                                          ]
[                                                          ]
[                                                          ]
[                                                          ]
[                                                          ]
```

What were or are the behavioral consequences of your beliefs?

How would you prefer to act or react? How could you behave more constructively?

```
[                                                          ]
[                                                          ]
[                                                          ]
[                                                          ]
[                                                          ]
```

What is your ultimate goal or desired outcome from changing these beliefs, emotions, and actions?

What are the negative, undesirable outcomes that have or will result from your feelings or actions?

```
[                                                          ]
[                                                          ]
[                                                          ]
[                                                          ]
[                                                          ]
```

What is the outcome or result you would prefer to experience in this current situation?

```
[                                                          ]
[                                                          ]
[                                                          ]
[                                                          ]
[                                                          ]
```

What is the outcome or result you would prefer to experience in the future if this situation was ever to happen again?

```
[                                                          ]
[                                                          ]
[                                                          ]
[                                                          ]
[                                                          ]
```

What else that you haven't yet identified would you have to change, do, or do differently in order to create this desired outcome?

```
[blank box]
```

F = Further Action > What do you need to do next?

Use the space below to identify ideas for activities or processes, whether from this course or elsewhere, as well as additional action steps you are going to take.

Activities or processes from this program I am going to use:
Activity/Process:

```
[blank box]
```

Date/Time I will complete them: _____

Action steps I am going to take:

Action Step:	Goal/Outcome:	Date/Time I will complete them:

Daily and Weekly Journal Prompts

The following are simplified journal prompts that can be used in addition to or instead of the complete ABCDEF Journaling process.

Journal Prompts for Reflecting on the Day

What went well today? Can you think of five things?

What was challenging for you today and what did you learn about yourself from that experience?

What did you enjoy about today? Can you think of particular experience or examples that made you happy during the day?

What are you grateful for? Can you think of 10 people or things that you have gratitude for today?

What do you want to feel tomorrow? What do you desire for yourself tomorrow?

Journal Prompts for Reflecting on the Week

Who made you feel good this week? What did they do or say?

```


```

What was the biggest mistake you made this week? What did you learn about yourself from this mistake?

```


```

How did you surprise yourself this week? Did you do something the old you would have never been able to do?

```


```

What did you do this week that moved you closer to reaching your goals?

```


```

Is there anything you did this week that you wish you'd done differently?

```


```

What did you enjoy doing this week?

```


```

What did you learn this week?

Additional Journal Prompts

What makes you unique (positive comments only, please)?

Write your body a letter thanking it for all it does for you (try not to be negative or body-shaming).

How do you want to be remembered and what do you need to do in order to be remembered this way?

Make a list of things you want to do before next year.

Make a list of your best character traits.

Make a list of your accomplishments, see if you can go through your life span and list 20.

What are you really good at?

How would your best friend describe you?

What would you do if you knew you could not fail?

Who are your role models and why? How are you on your path to be more like them?

What would with your time if money were no object?

If you could become an expert in any subject or activity, what would it be?

My favorite way to spend a rainy day is…

What advice would I have for my teenage self?

The three moments I will never forget in my life are… (Describe them in detail and why they're so unforgettable.)

What are 30 things that make you smile? (i.e., kitties)

My favorite words to live by are…

I couldn't imagine having to live without…

When I'm in pain of any kind, the most soothing thing I can do for myself is…

Make a list of the people in your life who support you and whom you trust. (Then make time to hang out with them.)

How would you define unconditional love?

How would you treat yourself if you loved yourself unconditionally? In what ways could you act on these things now?

If others really knew me they would know that…

What is <u>enough</u> for you?

If my body could talk, it would say…

Think about a way you have supported a friend or relative recently. How you can do the same for yourself.

What do you love the most about life?

What always brings tears to your eyes?

What were your first loves in life, such as favorite people, places or things?

What 10 empowering words best describe you?

What has surprised you the most, about yourself, related to your ability to thrive in life?

What lessons have you learned from your biggest mistakes?

When do you feel the most energized?

Make a list of everything that inspires you — including people, courses, websites, ideas, art, nature, whatever!

What's one thing you love to learn more about that would help you live a more fulfilling life? (Great! Now, go study it!)

When do you feel the most comfortable in your skin?

Make a list of the things that you've always wanted to say "no" to.

Make a list of the things you've always wanted to say "yes" to..

Write yourself a letter telling you what you've always wanted to hear.

Identifying Problem Areas

There are 7 common problem areas where many people's thinking and behavior holds them back from achieving their goals. You can complete this assessment when thinking about a specific goal you are working on but are having difficulty accomplishing, and then identify which areas are getting in your way. Alternatively, you can complete this assessment when thinking in general about what areas you primarily struggle with. The attached assessment will help you identify the problem areas, the thoughts, emotions, and behaviors that illustrate the problem, and point you toward sections and selections within this program that address that specific problem area. It's like a guide to making the most of the material in this course to help you overcome your roadblocks and move forward toward your goals!

The 7 Common Problem Areas Are:

1. Feeling limited due to not being good at something, perceived low level of ability or intelligence
2. Difficulty making a decision
3. Unable to get started or take action
4. Fear or resistance
5. Self-sabotage or procrastination
6. Negative self-talk and/or limiting thinking and beliefs
7. Stress, overwhelm, anxiety, obsessive thinking, or feeling out of control

Of course, there may be other problems you may be experiencing, so feel free to identify them here. There are also many additional situations that are addressed through the material in this program. As you work your way through the material, you will identify key activities that you find the most helpful for your purposes. This course is meant to provide a repository of insights and tools that you pick and choose from and apply them to the goals you set.

As you identify the areas you will be focusing on, celebrate the progress you have already made by taking the initiative to get to this point! There is no more meaningful work than learning how to use your mind to create your life!

Desired Goal: _____

Problem area:	Thoughts that illustrate the problem:	Emotions or behaviors that illustrate the problem:
Feeling limited due to not being good at something, perceived low level of ability or intelligence		
Difficulty making a decision		

Unable to get started or take action		
Fear or resistance		
Self-sabotage or procrastination		
Negative self-talk and/or limiting thinking and beliefs		
Stress, overwhelm, anxiety, obsessive thinking, or feeling out of control		
Other		

A = Activating Event

We're going to look deeper at the process for each step of the ABCDEF process, starting with A which stands for the Activating Event. Remember to return to the Simplified ABCDEF Form in the previous section to execute the process.

The sections in this section go along with the ABCDEF activity, and then the rest of the course sections provide additional processes for identifying and changing thoughts and beliefs for each of these steps.

Step 1: Identify the Activating Event:

What is the activating event? Basically, this means something that is happening that you don't like or that disturbs you. Describe or summarize the situation in a journal or other location where you'll be working through this process. (Note that this process can be used to reflect on an event that happened in the past, however the sooner this process is done after the event happened the more helpful it will be because the details of the experience and thoughts processes going on will be more accurate.)

Step 2: Get More Specific:

Is it real, such as an event or situation, or imagined, such as a thought or memory?
Is it past, present, or future?

Is it external, such as something happening to someone else, or internal, something happen to or inside of you?

Step 3: What Are You Experiencing?

What are you experiencing, emotionally? How do you feel?

What physical sensations do you notice (or were you experiencing at the time)?

How intense are these emotions and sensations on a scale of 1 to 10?

Step 4: What Are You Thinking?

What are you inferring about the situation? Basically this means what is your interpretation of what is happening?

What do you assume about it? (One way to identify this is to ask yourself, "what are my automatic thoughts about this? What is the voice in my head saying?")

How much did you believe in these thoughts and assumptions when you thought them? (On a scale of 1 to 10.) _____

Let's look at an Example:

Step 1: Activating Event: Your friend passes you in the street and doesn't say hello.

Step 2: Specifically, it's a real situation that just happened and you're experiencing it internally.

Step 3: You're experiencing feeling rejected and sad. There's a tightness in your chest. It's about a 7 on a scale of 1 to 10.

Step 4: You're thinking to yourself "He is ignoring me. He doesn't like me. I fear I could end up without friends." You believed those first 2 statements at a level 10 and the final one at a level 7.

As you can see, there are multiple things going on in this first step.

- The actual situation
- Your interpretation of it and thoughts about it
- An emotional and physical experience
- Your initial assumptions about the whole experience.

All of this happens in a quick moment and without us being aware that it's happening. To us, it feels like our automatic reaction to what is happening.

In the next step, we'll look a little deeper at the underlying beliefs that cause us to interpret situations the way we do. And then we'll look at the consequences we experience because of our interpretations, assumptions, and beliefs. But it's important to notice that the activating event itself is not what causes the consequences… the activating event (step A) triggers the beliefs (step B) which lead to the consequences (step C).

Also, another important thing to understand is that these ABC steps can also lead to a loop because the consequences that happen because of the first activating event and belief can become the next activating event that we then respond to based on our beliefs and lead to more consequences.

Once we get to D—Disputing we will be able to break the loop an create change.

B = Beliefs

The second step in the ABCDEF process is B, which stands for the Beliefs. As we discussed earlier, there are two types of beliefs.

First there are the judgments we make about what a situation means (such as demands, awfulizing, discomfort intolerance, and people-rating) and then there are the core irrational beliefs, which we've referred to as demands, musts or rules.

Step 1: Identify Your Evaluative Beliefs:

What does this mean?

| |
| |

Why is this happening?

| |
| |

Does it meet my expectations or rules?

| |
| |

What is wrong about this situation? Why is this wrong?

| |
| |

How do you feel about the fact that this is happening?

[blank box]

What does it say about you or the people involved?

[blank box]

Step 2: Identify the Type of Evaluative Beliefs:

Which category of dysfunctional beliefs do the answers to your questions fall under? By identifying what type of belief is going on, you can more easily identify which activities will help you change the belief.

- Demands, including musts, absolutes and should
- Awfulizing, including worst case scenario, catastrophic thinking, or that it's horrible
- Discomfort intolerance, including feeling like you can't stand being frustrated, uncertain, inconvenienced, or uncomfortable
- People-rating, including judging yourself or others as bad or unworthy

[blank box]

Step 3: Identify Core Irrational Belief (Demands/Musts):

Identifying the core beliefs can take a little digging and contemplation.

Start by asking yourself, which of my rules for how life is supposed to be are being broken:
Rules about myself and being approved of by others?

[blank box]

Rules about how other people must behave in order to be worthy?

[blank box]

Rules about how live is supposed to be—meaning if it's meeting my demands for living without discomfort, frustration, or inconvenience.

```

```

For help identifying the core belief or demand, as well as the more specific belief you're struggling with and the truth that will help you shift your belief, see the Core Belief Identification Chart.

RECAP: Let's look at what this would look like using the example from before. So, your friend passed you in the street and didn't say hello. You feel rejected. You assume he doesn't like you and you fear you'll end up with no friends at all.

Step 1: Now, your evaluative belief or what you believe this means is that "I'm not wanted as a friend, so I must be worthless. It would be terrible to end up without friends."

Step 2: You're awfulizing and self-rating.

Step 3: Your core belief that is being triggered is about APPROVAL. You believe that in order to feel worthy I must be approved of by every significant other at all times.

Next, we're going to look at the consequences of your beliefs about this situation. Sometimes you will not be clear about the beliefs until AFTER you identify the consequences. This is because by reflecting on how you feel about a situation and the behaviors you are doing because of the situation you can more easily identify WHY you feel and act that way, which is the core belief. You may need to come back to this step later.

C = Consequences

The third step in the ABCDEF process is C, which stands for Consequences. Regardless of what happens in life, we always respond in one way or another, whether healthy or unhealthy, positive or negative, taking action or not taking action. In every single case there is a consequence.

In fact, there are four levels consequences:

- Emotional consequences
- Behavioral consequences (reactions)
- Outcomes or results
- Secondary emotional consequences

It is important to remember here that these consequences are NOT caused by the situations in our lives, they are caused by the thoughts and beliefs we hold ABOUT the situations in our lives. We will continue to come back to this point over and over again until you truly believe that the ENTIRETY of your power lies in your choices for what you THINK, FEEL, and DO.

In fact, all of the consequences we just looked at are because of how you RESPOND to a life situation. This is good news because you are able to CHOOSE how you respond to every situation in life. That is, in fact, where the word responsibility comes from. It literally means "ability to respond". And, so as you continue to work through this process you will be taking responsibility for your thoughts, emotions, and actions, and therefore taking back control of your life.

Congratulations!

Ok, so we already mentioned that sometimes it is helpful to assess the consequences BEFORE we seek to identify and change the underlying core beliefs. There are two reasons for this:

First, sometimes it will be hard to gain clarity about the core belief and looking at how you feel about the situation and how you are responding to it will give you clues to what you would have to BELIEVE in order to be feeling and acting this way.

Second, sometimes looking at the hard truth of the dysfunction and damage your emotions and behaviors are causing to yourself, others, and your life, can be just the wake up call you need to have a strong enough MOTIVE to commit to changing your thinking.

Motive is, in fact, the root word in MOTIVation for a reason. In order to be motivated to change, you need to have a strong enough reason.

So, let's look at consequences in more detail.

Step 1: Unhealthy Negative Emotions:

What are the major unhealthy negative emotions that you are experiencing about this event?
(Remember, the unhealthy negative emotions are anxiety, depression, guilt, shame, rage, hurt, jealousy, envy)

How did you feel DURING the event?

What thoughts were you thinking that lead to this feeling?

How do you feel now ABOUT this event?

What thoughts are you thinking now that lead you to feel this way?

How do you feel about the future consequences of this event?

[ ]

What thoughts do you have about how this will impact your future?

[ ]

Step 2: Self-defeating Behaviors:

How did you react to the situation? What did you say? Do? Think?

[ ]

How have you responded to the situation since it happened up until now? How have you behaved? What did you say or do?

[ ]

Have you used any self-protective or over-compensatory behaviors, such as:
- Going out of your way to please people
- Overcompensating to make up for something
- Pushing yourself too hard
- Avoiding potentially challenging, uncertain, or unpleasant situations
- Working too hard or trying to prove your worthiness
- Trying too hard to control other people or situations
- Being rebellious in attempt at proving your autonomy

[ ]

Step 3: Outcomes or Results:

Like we've been trying to point out, the reason that all of this matters is that all of these thoughts, beliefs, emotions, and behaviors lead to real, tangible outcomes or results in our lives. Looking honestly at the repercussions of your actions will help you feel the sting of pain that will help you commit to following through on changing them.

So, ask yourself:

How has how you felt or feel about the situation impacted you? Others (who, specifically)?

What has happened because of how you felt?

Can you see how your emotions influenced your behaviors and actions? Which emotions are connected to which behaviors?

What have been the results or outcomes that occurred because of your actions or behaviors? Which behaviors have resulted in which outcomes?

What future consequences do you anticipate will happen if you continue with these emotions, actions and behaviors?

What will happen because of these outcomes?

[ ]

Step 4: Secondary Emotional Disturbances

Now that you've identified how your emotions have lead to your actions and how your actions have resulted in the consequences in your life, the next step is to ask yourself how you feel ABOUT these consequences. When we've discussed secondary emotional disturbances previously, we used examples such as feeling guilty about our actions or feeling anxious about our anticipated anxiety. At this stage, we're also going to look at the consequences of these secondary emotions.

Ask yourself:

Looking back at how you felt and acted during the situation, how do you feel ABOUT it?

[ ]

Looking at how you have behaved or felt SINCE the experience, or now, how do you feel ABOUT it?

[ ]

How do you feel about the results or outcomes that have arisen because of how you felt and acted?

[ ]

Imagining the future consequences that you anticipate will result from continuing these thoughts, emotions, and actions, how do you feel ABOUT the future?

[ ]

Once you've identified any problematic unhealthy secondary emotions, you can start this process over again, including going to B to uncover the beliefs that are leading to this secondary emotion.

In fact, you can also look at the negative consequences you have identified here and go back to A, using these consequences as the Activating Event. Again, this ABC process can be never ending loop.

However, if you address what is happening NOW, rather than waiting for it to spiral into a greater and greater problem, you can STOP this cycle by moving on to the DISPUTING phase, which is next.

Again, use the activities in the rest of the course to address each of the ABCDEF steps in more detail.

RECAP: Before you move on, let's look at that example we've been using.

Your friend passed you in the street and didn't say hello. You feel rejected. You assume he doesn't like you and you fear you'll end up with no friends at all. Your think this means you're worthless. It feels awful. Your need for approval has been triggered because you believe you must be approved of by everybody at all times.

Now it's time to assess the consequences of this belief.

- Emotional consequence: you feel depressed and worthless
- Behavioral consequence: you avoid people because you believe you're unworthy as a friend
- Result: you become socially isolated
- Secondary emotion: the isolation reinforces the beliefs and increases depression

D = Disputing, Part 1—Inferences

The fourth step in the ABCDEF process is D, which stands for Disputing. As we've mentioned, the disputing step is where true change is possible. Until we first identify our thoughts and beliefs and then DISPUTE them we have very little chance of changing how we feel, how we act, or the results we get in our lives.

Like we discussed, the ABC process can get stuck in a loop where our interpretations, emotional reactions, and behaviors continue to cause negative consequences that then become problems themselves. Now that you've evaluated the situation and your perception, emotions, and actions, as well as identified your core beliefs and looked honestly at the consequences of it all, you're ready to dispute those beliefs!

By disputing the beliefs you identified, you break the cycle. However, in order to create true change, you'll need to continue on to steps E and F next.

The good news is that often simply recognizing the beliefs that are at the core of how we feel and act allows us to view them differently because they are quite obviously irrational. However, actually changing the belief permanently or changing how we feel or act in situations takes practice and more extensive re-training of our thoughts.

That's why we address the D step in 4 of the following sections.

First, we'll dispute irrational thinking beliefs in general, by practicing unconditional acceptance, banishing approval-seeking behavior, and using Socratic questioning.

Then, we'll address the 3 levels of thinking, starting with inference. We'll learn how to question our interpretations and assumptions to shift our perspective.

Next, we'll address the second level of thinking—evaluations. We'll use a variety of strategies for changing how we evaluate situations and assign meaning, starting with turning our demands into preferences.

And last, we'll challenging the third level of thinking—our irrational beliefs and learn how to replace them with empowering ones.

But first, let's set a foundation for how to dispute these beliefs. Then, the rest of the activities will build upon this core process.

Step 1: Dispute Your Inferences, Assumptions, and Perspective

Go back and look at what you identified in A. You've already identified the activating event and how you're experiencing it. You should also have identified your initial thoughts or inferences about the situation.

Now, ask yourself the following questions:

How much did or do you believe these thoughts you held or hold about the situation?

```

```

Are they true?

```

```

What are you assuming?

```

```

Could you be wrong?

```

```

How else could you interpret this situation?

```

```

What is an alternative way you could think about this? Or, what could you say differently to yourself?

```

```

How much do you believe this new way of thinking?

[ ]

RECAP: Looking back at our example about the friend who passed you in the street without acknowledging you, your inference or assumption was that he was ignoring you and doesn't like you.

By questioning this interpretation, you realize you may be misinterpreting the situation and that there could be another reason for your friend's behavior.

D = Disputing, Part 2—Evaluations

Step 2: Dispute Your Evaluations

Go back and look at what you identified about your evaluations in B. You already identified what you believe this situation means and how you feel about it.

Now, ask yourself the following questions:

What are you demanding?
Must it absolutely happen that way or is it possible that it would not?

[ ]

What would happen if you didn't get what you wanted?

[ ]

What would this look like if you simply preferred it instead of demanded it?

[ ]

How would you feel about it?

[ ]

Are you awfulizing or catastrophizing anything? How terrible did/does it feel (scale of 1 to 10)?

If it feels like the worst case scenario, could it actually be worse?

In comparison to other things that are worse, is this really THAT horrible?

Now that you think about it, how would you ACTUALLY rate how bad this is on a scale of 1 to 10?

Are you avoiding discomfort or frustration because you feel like it's intolerable?

How terrible did you initially feel like this inconvenience or irritation would be?

Would it actually be that bad? Would you survive? Is it the end of the world?

Is it possible that not facing the discomfort or frustration could actually make things WORSE?

What would be the negative consequences of continuing to avoid it?

[ ]

Are you people-rating yourself or others?

Is it possible that the other person (or you) has a reasonable explanation for their behavior? What could it be?

[ ]

If the person (or you) made a mistake, is it possible that they will do better next time?

[ ]

If the person (or you) is insufficient in a certain area, does this mean they are insufficient in all areas?

[ ]

If the person (or you) is flawed in one way, does it mean they are defective or unworthy overall?

[ ]

If a person (or you) behaves in a way you believe is undesirable or bad, does it automatically mean they are a bad person?

[ ]

How would it benefit you and the other party if you accepted that all people are imperfect, yet capable of improvement?

```


```

So, again, looking at our example about the friend who passed you in the street without acknowledging you, your evaluative belief was that you are unacceptable as a friend, you'll never have friends again, and you're unworthy.

When you question this belief, you realize that it can't be true because you do, in fact, have other friends and it is reasonable to believe you will have friends in the future as well.

And, you recognize that even if you did not have friends that does not define the entirety of yourself as a person or determine your worthiness.

D = Disputing, Part 3—Core Beliefs

Go back and look at what you identified about your core beliefs in B. Using the Core Belief Identification Chart you identified which of the major musts that your beliefs fall under, which are APPROVAL, JUDGMENT, and COMFORT, as well as more specific beliefs. For each of the common core irrational beliefs we've addressed the TRUTH that counteracts the irrational belief. Use the document with the list of truths as a guide to help you shift your beliefs to be more rational.

Ask yourself the following questions for EACH of the irrational core beliefs you've identified:
What is the irrational core belief?

```


```

Why do you believe it? Why does this matter? (For example, you would ask yourself: why must I always get everything right? Why must everyone approve of me? Why does everyone have to love me?)

```


```

Note that there may not be a good, realistic answer to this question because the belief is illogical. Instead of seeking a real answer, ask yourself "what would happen if this didn't happen? Why would it matter? Continue to ask "why?" until you get to the core. Often the core answer will sound a lot like "because I would be worthless" or "because life wouldn't be worth living".)

What is irrational or illogical about it?

[ ]

What evidence can you think of that proves this belief wrong?

[ ]

How could you re-write the belief so that it would be based on TRUTH and be rational?

[ ]

And, again, looking at our example about the friend who passed you in the street without acknowledging you, your core belief was that you absolutely need to be loved and approved of by all people who are significant to you.

When you question this belief, you recognize that although being loved and approved of by everyone is highly desirable, they are not absolutely necessary.

You realize that not everyone is going to like you and you don't want to spend your whole life trying to be what other people want you to be.

E = New Effect

The fifth step in the ABCDEF process is E, which stands for the new desired effect.

In it's simplest terms, this step is about identifying what you want. The goal is to identify how you would prefer to feel, what outcomes you desire, and what changes you want to make to your behavior and actions. The way you will achieve this goal is to develop healthy, empowering RATIONAL beliefs.

By getting clear about your goals, you'll be ready to take the final step, which is to identify what further action needs to be taken.

In order to identify what you want, look back at what you've been working on in steps A through D.

Step 1: What is the activating event or situation you are focusing on?

What were your automatic thoughts and assumptions about it?

[ ]

How did you feel (what were your unhealthy negative emotions)?

How do you expect to be faced with a similar situation again in the future?

How would you prefer to feel (what are the healthy negative emotions you could shift to)?

How would you like to interpret the situation next time? How is this different from the first time?

How would you have to think differently in order to feel the way you want to?

How would making these changes impact you?

Step 2: What meaning did you assign to this event?

In what way were you using dysfunctional thinking?

How would you prefer to evaluate this situation?

What would you like to believe that this means?

What would you need to think or do differently to make this change?

How would making these changes impact you?

Step 3: Which core irrational beliefs, musts or rules are being triggered by this situation?

Which specific beliefs are at the core of what's going on here?

How could you change each of these specific beliefs to be more rational?

What do you want to believe?

How would making these changes impact you?

Step 4: What were or are the emotional consequences of your beliefs?

How would you prefer to feel about the situation?

Step 5: What were or are the behavioral consequences of your beliefs?

What dysfunctional or unconstructive behaviors or actions have you or are you doing?

How would you prefer to act or react? How could you behave more constructively?

Step 6: And finally, the last step is to identify your desired outcome.

What are the negative, undesirable outcomes that have or will result from your feelings or actions?

```
┌──────────────────────────────────────────────────────────┐
│                                                            │
│                                                            │
│                                                            │
│                                                            │
│                                                            │
│                                                            │
└──────────────────────────────────────────────────────────┘
```

What is the outcome or result you would prefer to experience in this current situation?

```
┌──────────────────────────────────────────────────────────┐
│                                                            │
│                                                            │
│                                                            │
│                                                            │
│                                                            │
└──────────────────────────────────────────────────────────┘
```

What is the outcome or result you would prefer to experience in the future if this situation was ever to happen again?

```
┌──────────────────────────────────────────────────────────┐
│                                                            │
│                                                            │
│                                                            │
│                                                            │
│                                                            │
│                                                            │
└──────────────────────────────────────────────────────────┘
```

What else that you haven't yet identified would you have to change, do, or do differently in order to create this desired outcome?

```
┌──────────────────────────────────────────────────────────┐
│                                                            │
│                                                            │
│                                                            │
│                                                            │
│                                                            │
└──────────────────────────────────────────────────────────┘
```

Looking back at our example about the friend who did not acknowledge you, you want to feel more confident. In order to feel more confident you would need to depend less on the approval of others for your sense of self worth., You want to believe your friend has a good reason for not acknowledging you, and so you would need to shift your perspective and assume that he did not notice you because he was distracted. And, you want to both reach out to your friend and continue to be social and develop strong friendships, and so you would need reach out, rather than withdrawing, and to develop a belief that even if this one friend did reject you, you are still a worthy person and a valuable friend.

F = Further Action

The sixth and final step in the ABCDEF process is F, which stands for Further Action.

This last step is about determining what actions to take in order to accomplish your goals, which are the new effects you determined in step E. Ultimately, this means identifying what you will do or not do in order to avoid repeating the same reactions the next time you are faced with a similar situation. This step is so important because this is where you take responsibility for creating lasting change.

So, the questioning you're asking is "what do I need to do next?"

The best way to identify what steps to take is to look at an example, so let's finish with the example we've been using about the friend who didn't acknowledge you.

Your goals are to feel more confident, believe your friend had good intentions, reach out to your friend, and continue healthy relationships in general. So, here are several steps to take in order to accomplish these goals:

Choose a positive interpretation to commit to, such as assuming he did not see you because he was distracted. If you find yourself resisting this belief and switching back to the original interpretation, write yourself an affirmation and post it somewhere you can see it every day, such as on a mirror or in your phone. Affirm to yourself "I know that my friend cares about me because he is always kind and has been there for me. I am sure he didn't say hello because he was distracted and didn't see me." If you need to, write out a giant list of reasons why you believe this.

In order to feel more confident and feel less dependent on approval, plan time this week to review the "truth" statements in the corresponding belief under the Major Must #1 APPROVAL belief. Review them one time every day for a week. Also, complete the Changing Limiting Beliefs activity this week.

After completing the first two activities your mindset will be prepared to face the situation with a new perspective. So, at this point reach out to your friend through a phone call or even an email if a phone call is not possible. If you feel it would be helpful, decide ahead of time what you would like to say. If you wish to address that you saw them, find a way to say it that does not sound accusatory. For instance, you could say "Hey! I saw you by XYZ store the other day." And then allow them to respond, "Really? I didn't see you, when was that?"

And lastly, continue to develop healthy friendships by practicing challenging your irrational demands, including the ones about approval. Commit to practicing the processes in this program to identify and change your thoughts and beliefs. Schedule time on the calendar every day for 1 week in order to commit to improving your ability to direct your own thoughts, beliefs, emotions, and behaviors.

Another option to build confidence would be to do one thing each day that you would normally avoid doing for fear of judgment or rejection. By practicing being vulnerable to disapproval and finding that even if someone does disapprove, you are, in fact, still alive and perfectly worthy, it will help you get over your irrational fear.

So, now, for each of your goals, identify 2 to 4 action steps that you need to take to move toward your goal and when you will take them. Putting a timeline on your actions and putting them into your calendar or setting reminders will keep you accountable. Of course, working with a life coach is always a great way to stay on track!

Step 1 (A, B & C): Identifying Activating Events, Beliefs & Consequences

Recognizing Emotional Disturbances

Sometimes people have a difficult time identifying their emotions and it's usually because of one of the following reasons:
- We were made to think our feelings don't matter
- We were made to fear expressing our emotions
- We were made to feel guilty if our emotions (or desires) were an inconvenience on others
- We were discouraged from feeling or expressing specific emotions

Because of our conditioning, some people stop expressing their emotions and often repress them (hold them in). Other people go a step further and stop allowing themselves to have them. In either case, this can lead to a lessened ability to recognize how they feel.

Even people who did not learn to repress or turn off certain emotions—even if they feel things deeply—they can simply not have ever been taught about their emotions and so they cannot clearly identify them. Their emotions feel overwhelming and out-of-control.

If you want to re-gain your power to direct your own emotional state, you need to be able to:
- Notice you're experiencing an emotional state
- Identify what it is
- Know what to expect
- Know how to influence a new emotional state

Emotional States

Emotional States are actually 2 different things:
1. The STATE is the physiological "feelings" that you experience
2. The EMOTION is the psychological interpretation or "label" you put on the state

We experience complex states made up of chemical and hormone interactions that cause a variety of reactions in the body. Our emotions are the interpretations we make of these experiences—or the labels we give them. So, based on what we talked about in Thoughts Create Emotions, we need to add a couple steps to the process.

Situation → Interpretation (thought) → State → Interpretation (label) → Emotion

What this means is the body responds to the thought first, then our minds interpret the reaction, label it, and an emotion is born. We can have physiological feelings that aren't emotions. We can feel hot, cold, nauseous, or energetic. But when we interpret them to have meaning, we turn them into emotions. Emotions literally mean action: e-MOTION. Each emotional state is designed to get us to do something, and often we do. Our emotional state affects our behavior, but it does not cause it. When we're angry we're more likely to be aggressive, but our cognitive (thought) processes allow us to make those decisions.

The Map is Not the Territory

The labels we give emotions are like a box or a map. What's printed on the box may signal what's inside, but it is NOT what is inside. Just like a map may describe a territory, however it is NOT the territory. Maps are simplified, inadequate and ultimately flawed. It would be like eating a menu. In the same way, what we call "anger", the word, is not the experience. Saying you "love" someone hardly does the experience any justice. In fact, all words are simply signposts pointing toward meaning. The word "tree" is not a tree.

So, what IS an emotion if it's not a map? Well, it's not a "thing" either. You see, labeling an experience as an emotion makes it seem like a NOUN. This is why many people believe emotions are things they HAVE or that happen TO them. The truth is that emotions are verbs (emoting is the verb)— they are a PROCESS. Fear is the process of fearing, which is a string of sensations that occur in a pattern. Fear takes many steps from observation or contemplation to processing and interpreting; then to physiological reaction and FEELING, and finally labeling it as fear.

Emotion Identification Chart:

Below are 6 common emotions and descriptions of the emotion, physiological state, and common resulting behaviors. This chart will help you get a general idea of the signs and symptoms of each emotion to make them easier to identify; specifically, easier to identify early. Everyone experiences each emotion somewhat differently and you may not experience all of the characteristics.

LABEL	EMOTION	STATE	BEHAVIOR
Happiness	Intense, positive feelings of well-being, pleasure, contentment, delight, joy, optimism, and gratitude. Affirmative, positive thoughts and mental clarity.	Head held high (posture), wide-eyed, smiling, laughing, relaxation of muscles, open body language.	Pleasant voice, friendly, swinging arms, dancing.
Boredom	Low-intensity, unpleasant feelings of apathy, restlessness, indifference, empty-ness, and frustration. Defeatist thinking or wishing things were different.	Low energy, slumped posture, smirk or frown, low eyes, shallow breathing.	Resting head, fidgeting, staring.
Anxiety	Vague, unpleasant feelings of distress, uneasiness, stress, apprehension, and nervousness. Thoughts of uncertainty and worry, racing thoughts.	Restlessness, sweating, clammy hands, hunched shoulders, swallowing, quickened breath, darting eyes, butterflies in the stomach, nausea.	Pacing, biting lip, fidgeting. Irritability, hypervigilance.
Anger	Intense, uncomfortable feelings of hostility and hurt. Feeling out of control. Thoughts of blame and resentment. Difficulty thinking clearly or rationally.	Muscle tension, headache, tight chest, increased heart rate, increased blood pressure, heavy breathing, clenched fist, furrowed brow, showing teeth, clenched jaw, sweating, trembling, flushed cheeks, large posture.	Loud voice, yelling, cursing, sarcasm, pacing. Sometimes leads to aggression, including hitting a wall, throwing an object, or lashing out at a person.
Sadness/Depression	Feelings of intense pain and sorrow, guilt, un-worthiness, disappointment, helplessness, gloominess, loss, grief, numbness, meaning-lessness, loss of interest. Defeated thinking and difficulty concentrating and remembering.	Slumped posture and hunched shoulders, long face, slow movements, pouting, body aches, crying, shaking, crossed arms, fatigue, upset stomach, monotone voice.	Curling up into a ball, laying around, withdrawing, irritability.
Fear	Intense feeling of dread, impending doom, or panic due to a perceived danger or threat. Paranoid or worst-case thinking and hyper focused on the object of the fear.	Increased heart rate, increased blood pressure, alert eyes, high eyebrows, corners of cheeks pulled toward ears, clammy, sweating, quickened breath, goose bumps, butterflies in the stomach, shaky voice.	Freezing, fleeing, hiding.

Practicing Emotional Awareness and Identification

Next time you catch yourself experiencing an emotion that is distinct, ask yourself the following questions. Practice this line of questioning often, especially when experiencing unpleasant emotions.

How do I feel?

How do I know?

What do I feel? Sensations?

Where do I feel it? Locations?

Where in my body did it begin? Move to?

How do I recognize when OTHERS experience this emotion?

Do I notice any of these signs in myself?

What do I observe in my body language, vocal tone, thoughts, behaviors?

Step 2 (D): Disputing Irrational Thinking, Beliefs

Unconditional Acceptance

The 3 core beliefs we've discussed all stem from a lack of acceptance. Lack of acceptance of:
- Yourself
- Others
- Life circumstances

These beliefs exist because we struggle to accept our reality because our reality does not meet our demands.

Ultimately, the only way to stop these beliefs from continuing to add emotional pain to life circumstances that are already challenging or make minor issues into major disturbances is to counteract the underlying problem. The solution is unconditional acceptance of what IS.

Just like the core beliefs are based on lack of acceptance of three things, the unconditional acceptance must be of all three. Which type(s) of acceptance do you need to work on the most?

1. Unconditional self-acceptance
2. Unconditional other-acceptance
3. Unconditional life-acceptance

Let's look at each of these forms of acceptance in greater detail.

Unconditional Self-Acceptance

This form of acceptance helps counteract the core belief about approval: I must be approved of by others to be worthy.

The reason people struggle with this is that they put unrealistic expectation on themselves. Then, when they don't meet their own expectations they beat themselves up for it. In order to accept yourself unconditionally, you must practice the following positive self-affirmations:

1. Nobody is perfect, including me. I have flaws just like everyone else, and that's okay.
2. One mistake or failure does not define me. I always have the ability to learn and improve.
3. My past does not define me. I am always able to make decisions for how I will think and behave today and into the future.
4. Being less-than ideal in one area does not define me or define my other traits or abilities.
5. Being perfect or having no flaws would not solve all my problems, make everyone approve of me, or ensure I always get what I want.
6. Having flaws or making mistakes does not make me less worthy than anyone else.
7. Other people's opinions about me are not accurate, because they don't know everything about me, and they do not determine my value or worth. In fact, other people's opinions don't impact me.
8. It is inevitable that not everyone is going to like or approve of me all of the time. It is more important for me to be authentic and approve of myself than it is to try to please others or earn their approval.
9. Although I enjoy being supported by others, I feel even more empowered when I take responsibility for myself and am free to do what I want, regardless of whether others assist me.

Being able to let go of this idea of perfection and truly embracing the perfection in our imperfection can shift many of the irrational thoughts that we have created about ourselves and what we think we should be. It also helps us grow because we can clearly and honestly look at areas that we want to grow, without judging ourselves or being overcritical of the areas that we are working on.

Unconditional Other-Acceptance

This form of acceptance helps counteract the core belief about approval: Other people must do "the right thing" and meet my expectations in order to be worthy.

The reason people struggle to accept others is almost always because of the way they perceive that the other person treats them or impacts them. We all want others to treat us a specific way—the way we define as "right". However, the reality is that we cannot control other people, how they act, or how they treat us. People are what they are and by telling ourselves that they're not supposed to be that way, and therefore judging them and being upset that they aren't meeting our demands, only gives us something to be upset about. And, by telling ourselves that we should be able to control other people not only causes ourselves irritation, it also leads us to behave in ways that cause problems with other people.

It is for our own greater good to accept that people are the way they are. This does not mean we have to accept unacceptable behavior or toxic people in our life. What it means is that we have to accept the reality that they ARE that way, whether we think they should be or not. By acknowledging this, we can then choose to disconnect from them or determine how to deal with the reality of the situation.

It is also important to realize that their behavior almost always has nothing to do with us.

Plus, someone's behavior does not define them as a person or determine their worth. For example, someone may react to us in a way we don't want, and so we judge their character. However, their behavior may not have had anything to do with you—they may have had just been having a really bad day. Plus, even if they acted rudely in this one situation, that would not negate all of their positive qualities as a person.

In order to accept others unconditionally, you must practice the following positive self-affirmations:
1. There will always be times that other people treat me unfairly, and even though I want them to treat me fairly, they do not have to do so.
2. Just because someone treats me unfairly does not mean that they are less worthy than anyone else.
3. Everyone has a reason for acting the way they do, even if I don't approve of their behavior.
4. It is not my job to control other people, however I am in control of my reaction to them.
5. It is no one else's job to meet my needs. I am responsible for taking care of myself, and this is a good thing because it gives me my power back.
6. There will always be people who have a different point of view or belief than me, and that is okay. They have reasons for believing the way the do.
7. If someone's behavior is unacceptable to me, I cannot change it but I can change my interaction with this person.
8. All people are multifaceted, so having a flaw in one area does not mean they are flawed in all areas.
9. All people make mistakes, so one poor choice, behavior, or failure does not mean a person is incapable or unworthy.

Unconditional Life-Acceptance

This form of acceptance helps counteract the core belief about approval: Life must be easy, without discomfort or inconvenience.

Many times, we want to control everything that happens in our environment. However, life is full of surprises. The surprises we don't like we call problems. However, when we accept that life is not perfect and does not unfold the way we always want it to we are open to truly finding the blessings in those unexpected situations. In fact, our biggest challenge can end up being our biggest blessings. However, they can only turn out to be our biggest blessings when we let go of the idea that life must be perfect.

1. Sometimes life's challenges and disappointments can lead to wonderful new possibilities that I never would have known I wanted.

2. No matter what happens in life, I know I am capable of finding a solution and that everything works out in the end.

3. There will inevitably be problems and situations that are outside of my control, however I always have control over my reaction to them.

4. I do not need to worry about potential problems because worrying does not impact the outcome. Instead, I can look for the positive aspects of the situation and seek rational solutions.

5. No matter what is happening around me or in the world, I always have a choice what I focus on, how I judge the situation, and how I react to it.

6. Often facing a challenge directly is the best method for finding a solution and feeling better.

Banish Approval-Seeking and Say No to "Should"

One of the 3 core beliefs is about the need for approval, and it leads us to judge ourselves and try too hard to gain approval of others. Approval-seeking is one of the most detrimental forces that leads a person to live inauthentically and out of integrity. Instead of making decisions based on what is best for them and instead of honoring who they truly are, they live their life for others—constantly adjusting themselves to be what they believe other people think they SHOULD be.

This approval-seeking behavior is so common that we don't even notice we're doing it. Some people have been people pleasing so long they don't even know who they really are. For me, my approval-seeking behavior started in 5th grade when a boy at my bus stop told me "Natalie, you always act like an animal." The truth is he was probably right. But form that point forward I was always concerned about not looking weird or being judged. Of course, that didn't stop me from being weird because I couldn't help it, and it didn't stop me from being judged… I was made fun of and bullied for many years.

For many people, the approval-seeking behavior starts with their parents. Their parents might be controlling and critical. They may also send mixed messages, for instances telling their child to choose what they want to wear, but then when the child makes their choice, the parent tells them their clothes doesn't match and make them go change. Constantly having their own preferences questioned or criticized leads to a child who, when asked by the store clerk, would you like a lollipop, the child looks at the parent, not because they're looking for the parent to give them permission, but to see if they even want the lollipop at all. They lose their ability to think for themselves. This, unfortunately, follows many people into adulthood.

There are a number of common approval-seeking behaviors, including:
- Changing your opinion at the first sign of disapproval
- Feeling anxious when someone disagrees with you
- Being unable to say "no" and so doing things for people and then resenting them for it.
- Being susceptible to sales people and tending to buy things you don't want
- Apologizing all the time
- Faking knowledge about a topic in order to impress others

If you relate to any of these things, you are not alone! In fact, approval-seeking is one of the most common afflictions! We all want approval and belonging. But the problem comes when we don't just want people to like us, we demand it. We NEED it. If you simply want approval, you're happy when people like you. But when you NEED it, you feel like you're going to die if you don't get it. Not only is this a problem because it is inevitable that not everyone is going to like or approve of you… but it's also a problem because it pushes you away from your true self.

Believing you NEED approval is like saying "your view of me is more important than my own opinion of myself." You sacrifice yourself for the opinions of others.

Think for a moment about a time when you were really upset that someone didn't agree with you or like you or approve of what you did. And now ask yourself, how would your life actually have been different if the person DID approve? In most cases, the truth is it wouldn't have made you any better off.

One of the areas where many people, especially women, tend to become preoccupied about seeking approval from others is how they look. People spend an absurd amount of money and time buying clothes that others view as "name" brand or high-end, cutting and dying and extending their hair, having fake nails installed, filling a closet with shoes, and painting their faces with makeup. Not to mention plastic surgery. When asked, many people say the reason they do it is because it makes them feel better about themselves, more confident. They want to look good. But what does that really mean? How does having perfectly quaffed hair, eyelash extensions, and $200 shoes actually make you a better person? Why would it make you more confident? You guessed it, because of what you believe OTHER PEOPLE will think about you because of it.

So, the question is, how would other people's approval or envy actually impact you? Does some random stranger looking at you and thinking you look sexy or rich actually mean anything? What would happen if they didn't think you looked great? How would that matter? Actually, if you think about it, in most cases you don't even know if anyone thinks you look great because they don't say anything. And then, when they do say something, often you're annoyed or offended! How much sense does THAT make?

How much energy do you spend wishing you were thinner, more muscular, had better skin, had better hair, had less of a neck glottal, had that new pair of shoes everyone wears these days? Would any of that really matter? And if not, isn't there something else MUCH MORE worthy of your time?

Now don't get me wrong, I think it's a great idea to seek approval of your behavior in the sense that you want to be a kind, considerate person and for people to recognize that. You don't want to denounce approval of others as an excuse to be a jerk and be like "I don't care what you think." But at the same time, you don't want to be a doormat and bow down to everyone else's desires and demands just so that they think you're nice. Be a good person, but honor yourself first.

The best way to decrease your approval seeking behavior is to practice getting other people out of your head. What I mean by that is to pay attention to the thoughts going on in your head, especially the ones that tell you what you should and shouldn't do.

When you tell yourself you shouldn't do something usually that "should" was told to you by someone else. So, whenever you hear that word "should" it's a sign that you're thinking someone else's thought or believing someone else's belief. The solution is to stop "shoulding" on yourself. Banish the word "should" from your vocabulary. When you hear that voice in your head urging you to do something because you "should", ask yourself:

Why should I do (or not do) this?

| |
| |

Who told me I should?

| |
| |

Do I truly believe I should?

| |
| |

In some cases, it will genuinely be something that you agree you should do 100%. In that case, make it a MUST for yourself and do it!

In most cases you'll recognize that you DON'T really believe you should do it and that you're only trying to make yourself do it because someone else's voice is in your head telling you should. Even if it's not a specific person, in general you are seeking to do what you should in order to gain approval. It's a bad habit, so be on the lookout for the world SHOULD and question any belief that is attached to it. Then, make your decision based on what YOU truly believe. When you do, you'll be living in integrity.

Stop Irrational and Illogical Thinking with Socratic Questioning

The truth is that we all think illogically or irrationally sometimes. I'm sure you know people who say things that you really wonder to yourself "how could they possibly think that?" Or, maybe you've had an argument with someone and it feels like you're spinning in circles or that you're talking to a brick wall. This happens because it's easy to get locked into a thinking pattern that doesn't make any sense. But the truth is that sometimes the person who is stuck in illogical thinking is YOU. Something can make so much sense to us at the time, but then someone points something out or you find our more information later that helps you realize that the way you were thinking about the situation made no sense.

When you're emotional, in fact, almost all thinking is irrational. The reason is that when we become emotional, our emotional center in our brain called the amygdala kicks on and floods our bodies with chemicals. At the same time, the prefrontal cortex, which is responsible for rational thought, shuts off. Our ability to think logically is literally impaired until our emotions are back under control. This is a really good reason for never making decisions when you're highly emotional AND why to never continue to talk or argue when either you or the other person is highly emotional. Nothing good will come out of it.

Sometimes, emotions aside, our thoughts are irrational because there are so many assumptions, distortions, and limited perspectives that can lead us not to be clear with our thinking. The good news is there are ways to root out illogical thoughts, which is important because if our thoughts impact our emotions and actions, we don't want to be creating our life experience based on thoughts that aren't true.

This is where Socratic questioning comes in, also referred to cognitive restructuring.

Socrates is an early Greek philosopher who was one of the greatest thinkers of all time. He was famous for his ability to prove that someone else's thinking was illogical. The person would state their opinion and then Socrates would ask them questions until he led the person to make a statement that contradicted their original claim, showing that their original opinion was illogical.

The philosophy behind this type of questioning is that disciplined questioning can help a person uncover the truth, expand their thinking, uncover assumptions, and follow a line of thought all the way through. You'll notice that this type of questioning is used in a number of activities in the program.

Thoughts are going on inside our minds all the time like a running dialog. They happen fast and we often aren't really aware they're happening. We have an entire section dedicated to developing awareness, but to start use this activity to begin tune into your thoughts. The attachment that goes with this section helps you use Socratic questioning on yourself to determine if what you are thinking is logical.

These questions will help you develop a greater understanding of WHY you think what you think and whether the thought is rational and logical. Then, later in the course we'll look at how to use this type of questioning to question underlying belief systems.

Socratic Questions

What is the thought you would like to question?

What evidence is there that this thought is true?

What evidence is there that is might not be true?

Is this evidence based on facts or your feelings?

Is your thinking black and white or all-or-nothing? Is the situation more complex than what you are assuming?

Could you be misinterpreting the evidence or making any unverified assumptions?

Would other people have different interpretations of the same situation? If so, what might they think?

Are you looking at ALL relevant evidence, not looking only at the evidence that supports what you already believe?

```




```

Are you exaggerating or thinking this way just because it's your habit?

```




```

Where did this thought came from? Who may have passed it onto you? Are they a valuable source?

```




```

Step 3 (D): Changing Your Perspective (Inference)

The Power of Perspective

We've already said it multiple times throughout this course... it is not the situations in our life that determine how we feel and the actions we take because of it... it is our PERSPECTIVE of the situation that determines how we feel and behave. What this really means is that if you are feeling terrible or you are doing something that is getting you results you don't want, you need to shift your perspective.

Part of the first step in the ABCDEF process is to identify how you are interpreting the situation or activating event. This usually means what assumptions and judgments are you making about the situation? Once you identify what you are inferring or the perspective you are taking of the situation you can dispute it—meaning you can find another way of looking at and interpreting the situation.

So, what is perspective anyway?

Imagine you're standing on the top of a hill, back to back with your friend. In front of you, at the bottom of the hill, is a collection of dilapidated homes. Their roofs are covered in tattered tarps from leaks that were never fixed. There are heaps of trash along the street, and a group of young children are running together in bare feet kicking a deflated soccer ball. Your heart hurts as you observe the extreme poverty that these children live in. You say to your friend, who is standing behind you facing the other direction, can you believe this? It's so sad!

Your friend responds, what do you mean? This is amazing! You're thinking to yourself, what? How could this be amazing? But then you realize that your friend is looking the other way. Your friend is seeing the world from a different angle or point of view. Your friend has a different perspective. You turn around to get a glimpse of what your friend sees from their perspective and you see a beautiful view of a sunset over a lake. Amazing indeed.

This example shows that every person has a different perspective in life and just because someone else believes something different than you do does not mean they are wrong—they are just seeing the world in a different way.

But an even more important aspect of perspective is when we INTERPRET the world we see.

This time, imagine you and your friend are standing atop the hill but this time you're both facing the dilapidated houses. Your response is still "can you believe this? It's so sad!" But your friend says to you, "I think it's amazing!" At first you're horrified. How could this be amazing? But then you decide to ask what they mean. Your friend replies, "It's amazing that even in such a terrible environment those kids are able to have fun and experience joy. I find it inspirational"

In this situation, both you and your friend are seeing the same exact circumstances yet your perspectives—or how you interpret the situation—are very different. In this case, you are making a negative inference. Your negative thoughts about the situation make you feel upset about it. Your friend, however, has positive thoughts about the situation and so feels great. The situation is not responsible for how either of you feel—your thoughts about it are responsible.

But it isn't even just that your thoughts were negative and your friend's thoughts were positive. Another factor that impacts your reaction to the situation is what you are ASSUMING about it. Your friend assumes that the children are happy, while you assume that they are unhappy, or at least you think they should be because, after all, you would be unhappy if you lived in those conditions.

So, this story shows that there are two ways your inferences can become problematic.
1. You can make incorrect assumptions about a situation
2. You can interpret situations in a negative way

First, let's look at assumptions.

No matter what is happening in our life or around us, there is always a limit to what we actually know about what is happening. We can't see what is happening that isn't right in front of us. We don't know what happened previously. We don't know much about the people involved and we definitely don't know what they think or feel. But our brains love certainty and always seek to form conclusions, and so we make assumptions about the situation. We specifically make assumptions about whether or not we believe the situation or people involved are meeting our expectations and demands.

Whatever we don't know, we fill in the gap. We make up a story to explain what we're seeing or experiencing so we can explain to ourselves what is happening.

Then we believe our conclusion about the situation is fact—that it is reality. But the truth is that we're almost entirely wrong.

Then, we use this perspective we have about reality to make our next judgment, which is the next step—we determine what we believe all of this MEANS.

All of this assuming and perspective-taking reality all happens automatically and in a split second.

However, once you become aware, either by noticing your emotional reaction, noticing what you're thinking or saying, or noticing the consequence of your point of view—such as how you acted in response—you can choose to reflect on what you were thinking about the situation that caused your reaction to it. Ask yourself:

What do I believe is/was going on?

What assumptions did I make about it?

Is my perspective true?

How do I know?

What do I not know for sure about the situation?

Could someone else have a different perspective of this?

What other ways could I look at this?

In what way could I choose to look at this situation in order to see the good, feel more positive about it, or find the silver lining?

This last question is important because the way we interpret a situation determines how we feel about it and how we feel ultimately determines our experience as well as our behavior. If the situation is what it is, which it always is, the first step is to try to interpret it rationally and accurately by recognizing that there is much we do NOT know about it. The second step is to find a way to look at it that focuses on the positive and helps us feel healthy emotions about it. Why does this matter? Because feeling bad about ANYTHING does not make the situation better. If you're going to have to be stuck waiting in line anyway, you might as well enjoy the experience, right? In the same way, if a situation is challenging, you might as well find an optimistic way of looking at it so that you feel hopeful and seek a solution rather than complaining, feeling sorry for yourself, and shutting down.

Choosing your perspective is one of the most powerful superpowers you have, and one you probably have not been using to its full capacity. The other sections in this section will help you shift your perspective and practice positive thinking.

Reframe Negative Experiences

Imagine each situation in life is like a photo in a frame. The frame that holds the photo influences how the photo appears. Other things around the photo also impact how you perceive it, such as the lighting, the color of the wall, or where it's hung. These differences can even change the meaning of the photo. A photo of an explosion that is hanging on the wall in an office building that says "blow up your limits" means something totally different than that exact same photo hanging on a wall in a war memorial museum. With any photo or situation in life, if you change the frame or the way you're looking at it, the meaning changes.

That's why we change our perspective of a situation, we call it "reframing".

The Power of Interpretation or Perspective

You may not always be able to change what happens around you, but you always have a choice of how you respond, react, and how you view the situation. The situation itself does not determine the outcome, your perspective does.

Even the worst experiences of life, that feel like a curse, can be re-framed to find the blessing contained within them. It is the MEANING we attach to a situation that determines whether it moves us forward or holds us back.

Practice Finding the Silver Lining

For every seemingly negative circumstance in life, there either was (or could be) a positive outcome because of it.

- If your relationship hadn't ended bitterly, you may not have the loving relationship you have today.
- If you had not been downsized during the recession, you may not have returned to school and changed your career.
- If you had never made mistakes, you never would have learned the lessons that made you who you are today.
- If you had never experienced loss of a loved one, you would not have the same appreciation for those in your life today.

The moral of the story is that you always have a CHOICE of to look for the silver lining in any situation.

Reframe Negative Experiences

When something happens that makes you frustrated, sad, angry, or disappointed, ask yourself the following questions:

What else might be going on here?

What did I learn from this experience?

[text box]

What can I do differently next time?

[text box]

What positive outcome eventually came as a result of this situation?

[text box]

What meaning does it have? What purpose does it give me?

[text box]

How can I use this for GOOD?

[text box]

Practice: Make a list of any experiences from your past that were "negative" and then identify the positive outcomes and/or the empowering lessons you can take from them.

Change Your Perspective and Your Words

The words you use are one powerful way to shift your perspective. For example, the word "fail" can conjure up strong emotions and fear. To someone with a fixed mindset, failure is the ultimate worst-case scenario because it means you ARE a failure.

By changing your perspective, you can change the way you view failure. Let's try it now.

The truth about failure is that as long as you learn something from it that you apply to your life, nothing is lost. It is only failure if you either don't learn from it and give up or if never try in the first place.

Imagine you wanted to climb a mountain. You're standing at the bottom looking up, feeling afraid that you might fail. But you are already in the failure position. Why? Well, because if you tried climbing the mountain and failed, you'd end up back where you are. So, not trying to climb the mountain is the same as failing.

There are also many stories of famous failures that illustrate how failure is not a death sentence. Walt Disney was fired from a job and was told he lacked imagination. Steven Spielberg was rejected by the cinematic school he applied to. But they didn't see their failure as a reflection on themselves, they saw their failure as a learning opportunity.

Using the analogy of the mountain to see that not trying is the same as failure takes the fear out of failure because you realize you have nothing to lose. Finding evidence that supports that failure is not a bad thing helps us remember to look for the silver linings and what can be learned.

Another step you can take is to change the words you use. For instance, next time you hear yourself thinking or saying the world "fail", replace it with "learn". The new word helps you re-frame the situation and remember to look for the lesson.

Here's another example: the next time you catch yourself thinking "I'm not good at this", always add the word "yet". This lets your mind know that although you may not have the ability, this does not mean you can't. By telling your unconscious mind that you can develop the ability, you have given it a command and it immediately starts to tune into finding ways for you to learn and grow. This is the power of your words to change your perspective.

What words do you tend to use to talk about failure, your weaknesses, or to put yourself down?

```



```

What words could you use instead?

```



```

Positive Thinking and Affirmations

Positive Thinking

When you're in the midst of having a negative thought and the associated negative emotion it can be really hard to think positively. Even if the negative thought is faulty or untrue, it feels so right and real in the moment.

Positive thinking isn't about fooling yourself, it's about thinking MORE positively than your current negative state. That's why it's important to practice improving your thoughts, gradually. You see, the thought has momentum, like a car rolling down a hill. If you try to jump out in front of it and force yourself to change your thought, it will run you right over.

If you're thoughts are telling you "I'm unworthy", trying to tell yourself "I am powerful and amazing" may sound ridiculous to yourself at the time. It's unbelievable. Instead, you need to slow it down with incrementally better thoughts. Instead of reaching for the best thought ever, just try to reach for something a little better that feels believable to you from where you are. For instance, start with "I matter to a few people" and then "I have done important things in the past" and work your way up to "what I do with my makes a difference to others" and finally to "I matter".

Another way to counteract negative thoughts is to be preemptive. Instead of waiting until you're in the midst of a powerful negative thought to try to change your mind, practice positive thoughts ahead of time. Doing this can reprogram your thoughts and prevent those negative thoughts from happening, and when they do they are less powerful.

This process, often called affirmations, is the most effective when used for negative thoughts that you have regularly.

Affirmations

Affirmations are written or spoken positive statements that, when consistently practiced, rewire our thoughts and beliefs.

If you have a repetitive negative thought that causes you to feel bad, you can replace it with an empowering thought. If you repeat it to yourself regularly, such as when the negative belief is triggered AND at pre-determined times of the day, you practice this new belief, helping it become ingrained into your implicit, automatic, memory. Over time this thought becomes habituated and you BELIEVE it.

After you have created your affirmations, the next time you catch yourself thinking one of those repetitive negative thoughts, you can remind yourself of the new positive thought you've created to replace it. Because it's something you do repeatedly, using this new thought helps slow the momentum of the negative thought much faster than the first method we discussed.

The 4 P's for Successful Affirmation Statements:

- Personal (I, Me statements)
- Passion (put emotion into it)
- Present (as if it's already happening, not future)
- Positive (avoid words like "not" or "don't")

Lastly, you must repeat it REGULARLY.

Affirmation Activity:

For this activity you can focus on one thought you are looking to counteract, or you can brainstorm a number of different repetitive thoughts. What NEGATIVE BELIEFS to you commonly think to yourself (or even say out loud) about yourself, your capabilities, your confidence, or anything else that holds you back?

For each negative belief, write a NEW phrase that is positive and empowering, using the guidelines above. Ask yourself, what would counteract the negative thought—nullify it? What would be the opposite? What do you WANT to think or believe in this situation?

Common Negative Belief	New, Positive Belief

112

Repeat this affirmative statement at least 3 times a day (5 to 10 times each session). Consider posting it on your mirror, computer or nightstand where you can see it regularly.

The next activity uses a similar process to identify the lies we tell ourselves or the negative thoughts we think about ourselves and replace them with the truth!

113

Step 4 (D): Changing the Meaning You Assign (Evaluations)

Changing Your Evaluative Thinking

So much of what we experience as a reaction to life happens on autopilot, including our initial thoughts, assumptions, emotions, and initial behaviors. It can be challenging to even notice what we are thinking, feeling, or doing in the moment. But how we evaluate what all of that means is a cognitive process that is a little easier to become aware of. This is why we have said that our EVALUATIONS is the point in this process where we hold the most power to change our thinking. Whether we catch ourselves having a negative reaction to something in the moment or we're reflecting back on it after the fact, once we are aware there is a problem, the MOST IMPORTANT question to ask is—what does this mean?

The goal is to identify how we initially assign meaning and then to question ourselves in order to change the meaning we assign.

Earlier in the course we talked about evaluative thinking and the 4 dysfunctional ways we tend to assign meaning. In this section we're going to look at how to shift how we evaluate what a situation means by turning these dysfunctional ways of thinking upside down.

First, we'll address demandingness by looking at how to turn our demands into preferences.

Then, we'll address our tendency to awfulize and make things appear worse than they are with several activities meant to help you overcome worry.

We'll also look at our tendency to people-rate as well as how to develop a tolerance for feeling uncomfortable and embracing uncertainty.

The activities in this section address different aspects of evaluative thinking and can be used depending on what areas you are struggling with the most.

Turning Demands into Preferences

You'll remember that when we talked about what causes emotional disturbances, what was really going on was that we had placed demands on ourselves, others, and the world. Because our demands weren't met we evaluated the situation (such as awfulizing) and had a negative emotional response to it.

Our unreasonable demands, musts, needs or expectations are what cause our emotional disturbances. The solution is to tame our demands so we don't have such an emotionally charged response to them. We need to downgrade our demands to preferences.

If what you prefer doesn't happen, it doesn't feel like the end of the world. But when your demand or need isn't met, it feels absolutely terrible. By shifting our desires for the way we want things to be to be preferences, not needs, we are better able to cope with not getting our way.

Here is a process for turning demands into preferences. Identify your irrational belief and then identify the alternative to this belief, which is a preference. Refer to the Irrational vs Rational Beliefs section for examples of the difference between the demand (which is the irrational belief) and the preference (which is the rational belief).

My Demanding Belief:	My Alternative Belief (Preference):
Example: "I must be approved of by my girlfriend's parents" False | Illogical | Unhealthy	*Example: "I would like my girlfriend's parents to approve of me, but it is not mandatory." True | Sensible | Healthy*

True or False True or False
Write down your reasons or evidence to support your decision of true or false for each belief.

Logical or Illogical Logical or Illogical
Write your reasons or evidence to support your answer.

Healthy or Unhealthy Healthy or Unhealthy
Write down your reasons or evidence to support your answer.

Which of the two beliefs do you want to strengthen and act on? Demand Preference

Write down your reasons or evidence to support your answer.

Demand	Preference

True or False True or False
Write down your reasons or evidence to support your decision of true or false for each belief.

Logical or Illogical   Logical or Illogical
Write your reasons or evidence to support your answer.

Healthy or Unhealthy   Healthy or Unhealthy
Write down your reasons or evidence to support your answer.

Which of the two beliefs do you want to strengthen and act on? Demand Preference

Write down your reasons or evidence to support your answer.

Demand	Preference

True or False   True or False
Write down your reasons or evidence to support your decision of true or false for each belief.

Logical or Illogical   Logical or Illogical
Write your reasons or evidence to support your answer.

Healthy or Unhealthy   Healthy or Unhealthy
Write down your reasons or evidence to support your answer.

Which of the two beliefs do you want to strengthen and act on? Demand Preference

Write down your reasons or evidence to support your answer.

De-catastrophizing (Overcoming Worry)

This tool is great for talking yourself out of worrying or expecting the worst-case scenario, such as when you're making a big hairy deal about something. By looking at the facts of the situation it helps you reign in your exaggerated thinking and look more rationally at why this is happening.

What is the Catastrophe? Begins by identifying the catastrophe that you are worrying about. You should clearly state the predicted catastrophe and avoid using "What if...?" statements.

How Terrible is It? Also, rate how terrible you believe this catastrophe will be on a scale from 0% (not so bad) to 100% (absolutely awful). _____

How Likely is It? Once you have identified the catastrophe that is worrying you, ask yourself, "how likely the event is to actually happen?" Ask yourself whether a similar event has occurred in the past and, if so, how often it did it occur?

With the frequency of this previous catastrophe in mind, make an educated guess of how likely it is to happen. On a scale of 0% to 100%? _____

What is the Worst that Could Happen? What is the worst-case scenario? What is the best-case scenario? What is the most likely outcome? Try to put yourself in a friend's shoes and think about what you would say to yourself about your worry.

How Would You Cope? Once you have a good idea of how bad the catastrophe would actually be, ask yourself, "how would I cope with the fallout?" Note whether this has come to pass before and, if so, how you coped when it happened. Consider the resources you have at your disposal to help you cope, including friends and loved ones, skills or abilities you have, and methods or techniques that help you cope in other situations.

How Can You Reassure Yourself? Finally, you are directed to put together a narrative about the "catastrophe" based on the work you have done. Think about what you would like to hear in order to feel reassured, and what kind of tone would be most helpful. Once you have come up with something positive and reassuring to say to yourself about the potential catastrophe, rate how terrible you think the catastrophe will be once again.

Step 5 (D): Changing Underlying Beliefs

Challenging Irrational Core Beliefs

Once you've used the processes in steps AB and C and identified a core irrational belief, you can dispute it. This part is ultimately what the entire process has been leading up to because identifying the root of the problem—the core belief, rule, or demand—and shifting it to a rational belief is the key that unlocks lasting change.

This is exciting news, but you also need to keep in mind you may have spent years nurturing this belief and convincing yourself it is true. Some limiting beliefs don't let you rip them out by the root easily. It takes practice and persistence to change a core belief and develop an empowering belief that will serve you long term.

The best way to accomplish a belief shift is to wear it down through repetition. That is why this activity is meant to be done EVERY DAY. We recommend committing to this process daily for 14 days.

Set aside 10 minutes every day to identify a core irrational belief and ask yourself these questions. You may have identified a number of core beliefs during your other activities. You can also reflect on your day and identify any problems that came up and identify the core belief that lead to your disturbance.

When doing the activity, make sure you write down your answers. You can even record yourself instead. The reason this is so important is because your mind will try to pull you back into believing the old limiting belief. It has a habit of thinking that way and it will be easy to fall back into it. By writing it down, you can re-read your answers to remind yourself that the belief is irrational in those moments of weakness when it's tempting to believe it again.

Here are the questions:

What self-defeating irrational thought do I want to let go from my life and dispute?

Is my belief logical? Why or why not?

Is there evidence that disproves or counters this belief system?

119

Is there any evidence that shows this belief system to be true?

[ ]

Is this belief productive? Where or what is it getting me?

[ ]

Is it harmful to me?

[ ]

What is the worst-case scenario if I do NOT get what I think I must (or if I get what I do NOT want)?

[ ]

What positive things might happen if I do NOT get what I think I must have (or if I get what I do NOT Want)?

[ ]

What is a rational belief that can replace the irrational one?

[ ]

If you continue to practice questioning your core beliefs consistently, they will lose their power. Not only will your brain start to truly believe the new, rational belief, it will get better at spotting irrational beliefs in your every day life. You'll get so good at questioning your beliefs that you'll notice your emotions and behaviors throughout the day and automatically identify the core belief and challenge it right on the spot! Imagine how much heartache and stress this could save you!?

The last step is to be accountable! In order to reinforce your habit of disputing the irrational beliefs, determine a way you can reward yourself. For instance, you can choose an activity you enjoy, such as a hobby, socializing, or anything else you enjoy. Every day, after you complete this exercise, do the enjoyable activity as a way of rewarding yourself. This will help you associate disputing your beliefs with a positive emotional response, which helps reinforce the behavior.

How will you reward yourself?

Changing Limiting Beliefs

The Table Leg Method

Imagine your belief is like a tabletop and the evidence that supports your belief is like the table legs. You look at the evidence and make a conclusion—a belief about it. Just like with a table, if you knock enough legs out from under it the belief will collapse. You do this by creating doubt about your evidence or looking at it in a different way. Then, after you collapse the old, unwanted belief that makes you doubt yourself or your dream, you can use the same method to build up a new one. That's right, it works in reverse! If you determine a belief that is more empowering that you'd prefer, you can find evidence that SUPPORTS your new belief. Add at least 3 legs and the table will stand.

For example, if you believe that you are bad at math, you may have several reasons for this belief. First, it seems to run in your family. In fact, your mother said it's in her genes. This plants the first seed. Then, in 5th grade you got a math answer wrong when you were asked to do the math problem on the board in front of the class. It was embarrassing and reinforced your belief, making you thing "geeze, I guess mom was right!". Then, you failed the last two tests you took in your high school algebra class. You felt bad about it. Now the belief is stuck.

But believing that you are innately bad at math will hold you back. First, because you expect to do poorly you'll be more nervous when you take math tests, you'll be less likely to try harder or practice since you believe you're simply unable to do math. You will unintentionally prove yourself correct. This is called a self-fulfilling prophecy. In the end, you'll avoid things that you might have enjoyed simply because you expect they'll involve math and you don't want to do it because you think you're bad at it. Maybe you love science, but you never pursued a career in science because you didn't think you could do the math. Maybe you wanted to start a business but didn't think you could handle the finances because of your math deficiency.

When we hold limiting beliefs, they hold us back from our potential.

The good news is even the more strongly held beliefs that hold up the overall belief can be undone. The key is to question the evidence we use to support it, remove the superglue, and find a new, more empowering belief to replace it with.

Before we begin, it's important to understand that when we're talking about limiting beliefs, we are not saying that the belief is FALSE. It may be true or based on things that really happened. But whether it's true or false isn't the point. We're looking at beliefs that are either empowering or disempowering. They're either useful or harmful.

5 Step Process for Changing Limiting Beliefs

STEP 1: Identify a limiting belief you would like to change: Make a list of all of the things you can think of that provide evidence (table legs) that support your belief (at least 3 pieces of evidence).

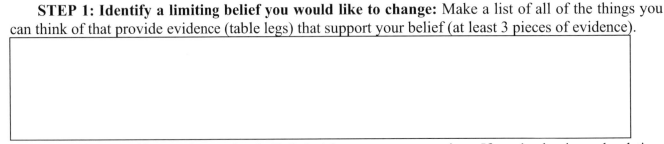

STEP 2: Identify an alternative belief that is more empowering: If you're having a hard time identifying a more empowering belief, ask yourself "what if I believed the opposite"? You want to choose a new belief that is believable. So, instead look for an IMPROVED belief. So, that could be "there is always opportunity in the market if you provide an exceptional product or service."

[Empty box]

STEP 3: Unstick the emotional superglue: Sometimes we become emotionally attached to our limiting beliefs. We experience benefits or emotional payoffs for keeping our limitations around, which makes them sticky. It is like super-gluing the table legs to the floor.

What is the emotional payoff for holding onto this belief? Be honest with yourself. Write down everything you can think of that may be an emotional or practical benefit.

[Empty box]

Step 3: Emotional Payoffs/Evidence	Step 4: Create Doubt

Next, ask yourself: do these benefits outweigh the costs of keeping this limitation? __Yes __No

- If your answer is YES—that the emotional payoff is worth it—then you will most likely NOT be able to change this belief because you are too attached to it.
- If you answer is NO—the payoff is NOT worth continuing to be limited by this belief—well, then it's time to celebrate because you've just dissolved the superglue! You actually WANT to change, and that means it's time to start dismantling that table.

STEP 4: Create doubt by reframing your evidence:

Like we said, you believe what you believe because you look at the evidence and come to a conclusion. But what if the evidence was wrong, incomplete, or you just weren't seeing it clearly? That would make you question your conclusion, and that's exactly the point of this step. For **each piece of evidence (emotional payoffs above)** you identified for your limiting belief, ask yourself the following questions (in the box above):

- Could this be untrue?
- Is there more to the story?
- What is an alternative explanation?

The point is to question the evidence enough to create doubt. Some evidence will be harder to refute than others, but that's okay as long as you can knock out enough to leave less than 3 legs standing!

STEP 5: Find evidence to support your new belief:

Now we're gong to flip this around and build up the supporting evidence to solidify your new belief. Looking back at your desired belief, make a list of everything you can think of that supports this new belief. You only need a minimum of 3 but you want to create as many legs as possible so that this belief is way stronger than the old, limiting one.

What supporting evidence is there to support your new, desired belief?

With enough supporting legs, your new belief will stand. It might not be as strong as your old belief at first, but that is okay.

In many cases, the table legs that held up your old belief may have been really thick or really super-glued because of the emotions tied to them. When thinking about evidence for your new belief, it may be harder to find emotionally-charged evidence, so you want to think of as many things as you can. The number of supporting legs will make up for the less powerful examples.

Uncovering the Lies

When you are completing this activity, focus on one category at a time.
Materials you'll need:

- 1 pen
- 1 pencil
- 10 sheets of lined paper (as many as you need)

How to Uncover the Lies and Rewrite Them

Step 1: Identify the Lies

1. Start with your pencil. Write down a lie your inner critic tells you about yourself.
2. Staying in the same life category, write down another lie.
3. Once you've exhausted beliefs in this category, move onto another category and repeat.

For example:
I'll never get married.

Step 2: Tell the Truth

1. Put away your pencil and take out your pen.
2. On the line under each lie, you're going to write the truth. The truth could be the opposite of your lie or it could be simply something nicer. Reach for the highest level, self-affirming belief you can find. *NOTE: Make sure your truth is written as a positive statement. Do not use "not" or "no" or "isn't" or "don't". For example, if your lie was "I am stupid" your truth would not be "I am NOT stupid" it would be "I am intelligent at many things".*

Step 3: 7 Daily Reminders

1. Next, read the lies and the truths to yourself every day for 7 days.
2. On the 7th day, ERASE the lies.
3. Revisit this activity any time you need a pick-me up, a reminder, or if you discover there are more limiting, critical beliefs you want to uncover and replace.

Activity sheet on the following page.

Lie (write in pencil):
Truth (write in pen):
Lie (write in pencil):
Truth (write in pen):
Lie (write in pencil):
Truth (write in pen):
Lie (write in pencil):
Truth (write in pen):
Lie (write in pencil):
Truth (write in pen):

Steps 6 (E & F): Determining the Desired Effect, Taking Action & Creating Change

Identifying What You Want

So, what do you want? If you're like most people, this is surprisingly difficult to answer. Most people are so inundated with messages from their parents, peers, and society of what they "should" want that their true desires are drowned out. Plus, even if they've held dreams and desires in the past, their life experiences have lead them to believe that what they want is not possible, and so they stop allowing themselves to want it. They tell themselves "I can't have that" and it hurts to want something they cannot have, and so they stop thinking about it. They give it up. They settle.

But the good news is that dreams can never die—deep down you know what you want. It tugs at you from within, but you may be so used to ignoring it that you no longer notice.

Forgotten Dreams

What do you REALLY want? Answer this without allowing other people's opinions or beliefs to limit you. Answer this without thinking about limitations—imagine for a moment that money is not an issue and that whatever that is currently blocking you is magically taken care of.

What are things you wanted, desired or dreamed about that at some point you decided you could NOT have and so stopped wanting them?

This could have been in childhood or adulthood. You may not have allowed yourself to think about these desires in a long time. For each one, ask yourself if this is something that you STILL want. If not, cross it out and let it go. Circle any desires that you feel a strong emotional reaction to when you think about them.

Identifying What You Do NOT Want

For many people it's easier to identify what they do NOT want than what they DO want. When asked what they want, many people respond "not this!" So, to start, simply make a list of the things you know for sure you do NOT want in your life. These can be things that USED to be in your life that you never want to experience again. They can be things CURRENTLY in your life that you would like to stop. They can be things you are simply certain you never want in your FUTURE.

Once you know what you do NOT want, it will help you identify what you DO want. Ask yourself, "What is the opposite of what I don't want?" or "If I know I do NOT want _____, then it means that I do want _____."

I do NOT want:	I DO want:

Getting More Specific

You have determined some things you want and don't want. You have determined the roles, beliefs and ego states that have influenced your life story and the new perspectives you can now take of them. Now, it is time to delve into greater detail about what you WANT your life to be. You can always add to this activity later, as you learn more about your desires. Later you will rewrite the story itself, but here you are asking yourself what you want in your life and why.

Area	What do I want?	Why do I want it?
Home		
Partner/ Relationship		
Family		

Career		
Leisure		
Money		
Health		
Other		

"Yes, I want more of this!"

Once you begin asking yourself about what you want, you'll find yourself noticing more and more things that make you think, "yes, I want this!" It's okay if you're still not sure what you want. Allow your desire to grow over time. Throughout your day, simply notice whether you like or dislike certain things, people, situations or experiences.

Say, "Yes, I want more of this!" to the things you like.

Say, "No, thank you." to the things you do not like. Saying "thank you" acknowledges that you appreciate the ability to identify what you don't want because it helps you know more clearly what you DO want.

Digging Deeper into "Why"

Now we're going to ask you to dig deeper into the answers you provided in the "why" column. This is important because only if you have a *big enough reason* will you be committed to creating lasting change. And, the only way your reason to change your life will be big enough is if you understand your core reasons. Below is an example that will help illustrate the point.

A student in one of our classes once told us, "I can't wait to go home and start using these efficiency techniques to make my work more effective and productive" And so we asked, "Well, why do you want to be more productive?" The student said that it would help her to get a promotion at work. We asked her why she would want a promotion and she said "So I can get a raise." So we asked again, "Why do you want a raise" and she said "Because I need the money to buy a larger home". So we asked "Why?" and she says because I want my mother and sister to move in with me". "Why?" "Because it has been our dream to own a big house together and live together as a family."

To which we responded, "Good, NOW you have identified what you really want. It's a large house with your family living with you. You don't really want to be more efficient. What you want is the experience of having your family living with you."

Look at the reasons you wrote for "why" and ask yourself the following questions:

My "Why" from Above:	Dig Deeper
	Why does this matter to you? Why? How would it make you feel? What would happen if I didn't have, do, or be this? Why does that matter? Why?
	Why does this matter to you? Why? How would it make you feel? What would happen if I didn't have, do, or be this? Why does that matter? Why?
	Why does this matter to you? Why? How would it make you feel? What would happen if I didn't have, do, or be this? Why does that matter? Why?
	Why does this matter to you? Why? How would it make you feel? What would happen if I didn't have, do, or be this? Why does that matter? Why?

Keep probing and asking yourself until you get to the core of the issue.

In some cases, you will find that your deeper motive is a specific desire, like in the example above. However, often the core motivation beneath your desire is actually an emotional state that you wish to experience. In fact, everything we want is because we believe it will make us *feel* the way we desire: good, or at least *better*.

Get Other People Out of Your Head

Lastly, consider if any of the things you "want" are truly only because you think you "should" want them. It's easy to unknowingly adopt other people's dreams. Get other people's voices and beliefs out of your head. Whose voice do you tend to hear in your head, telling you what you "should" want?

Now, look back at desires and confirm they are TRULY what you want and you are not just telling yourself to want them because someone else's voice is telling you that you should.

The Pain/Pleasure Principle

Everything we do in life is because we're either avoiding pain or moving toward pleasure. If you're continuing a pattern or behavior that you don't like, it's because you're linking more pain to stopping it than you are to continuing it. And if there's something you're not doing that you want to do, it's because you link more pain to doing it than not doing it. Below is an activity that will help you stop patterns and change behaviors because you associate massive pain to continuing the old pattern and you associate massive pleasure to the desired behaviors. List 4 patterns or behaviors that you need to change in order to reach your goals/dreams and the desired new behavior or outcome:

1) Unwanted Pattern:

Desired Outcome:

2) Unwanted Pattern:

Desired Outcome:

3) Unwanted Pattern:

Desired Outcome:

[text box]

4) Unwanted Pattern:

[text box]

Desired Outcome:

[text box]

Now for each desired change, answer the following questions:

PATTERN 1:
What is the PAIN you associate with stopping the old pattern or behavior?

[text box]

What is the PLEASURE you've gotten from doing the pattern or behavior?

[text box]

What is the PAIN that will happen if you DO NOT stop the pattern or behavior?

[text box]

What is the PLEASURE you will experience if you DO stop the pattern and create the desired outcome?

```



```

PATTERN 2:

What is the PAIN you associate with stopping the old pattern or behavior?

```



```

What is the PLEASURE you've gotten from doing the pattern or behavior?

```



```

What is the PAIN that will happen if you DO NOT stop the pattern or behavior?

```



```

What is the PLEASURE you will experience if you DO stop the pattern and create the desired outcome?

```



```

PATTERN 3:

What is the PAIN you associate with stopping the old pattern or behavior?

```



```

What is the PLEASURE you've gotten from doing the pattern or behavior?

```



```

What is the PAIN that will happen if you DO NOT stop the pattern or behavior?

```



```

What is the PLEASURE you will experience if you DO stop the pattern and create the desired outcome?

```



```

PATTERN 4:

What is the PAIN you associate with stopping the old pattern or behavior?

```



```

What is the PLEASURE you've gotten from doing the pattern or behavior?

```



```

What is the PAIN that will happen if you DO NOT stop the pattern or behavior?

```



```

What is the PLEASURE you will experience if you DO stop the pattern and create the desired outcome?

Exposure Techniques for Overcoming Fear and Resistance

Often the best way to overcome anything that you resist or are afraid of is to expose yourself to it in a way that gently gets you used to it. You can accomplish this gradual desensitization effect both mentally and in real life.

Imagery Based Exposure: The mind does not know the difference between reality and what is happening in the mind. Whether a situation is happening or you're imagining or remembering it, the brain reacts the same by producing the neurochemicals that make you feel an emotional response. This means that if you are afraid of something, whether it's public speaking, bringing up a difficult conversation, or riding in an airplane, you can use visualization to practice exposure mentally. This tool can also be used to practice a new skill or make a life change. Change can be scary, so using visualization is one way to overcome resistance by getting used to the experience ahead of time. You can work through the intimidating parts in your mind and play out all of the different options so that you know ahead of time how you want to react when it comes time for the real experience. Skills can also be practiced using visualization because imagining executing the skill or steps in great detail helps the brain create a habit of thought. Then, when you take the steps in real-life, it doesn't feel new, it feels like you've done this before.

Regardless of the situation you wish to expose yourself to mentally, determine what the experience would look like. Would there be steps to take? What would be going on around you? Who would be there? Sit down, close your eyes, and imagine the experience from start to finish. Imagine every step in great detail. When you experience a negative emotion of resistance or fear, observe how it feels. Ask what you are thinking about the situation that is making you feel that way. Ask yourself what you would want the experience to look like in order for you to feel more comfortable with it. Then, continue imagining the experience going well. Imagine yourself feeling comfortable and content. You can even add fun or relaxing elements to the scene if you want, such as music or color. Imagining the situation with these added elements helps program the mind to expect to feel good when the situation happens in real life. You may need to do this activity several times until you can go through the entire process feeling good.

Situation Exposure Hierarchies: Another way to gradually expose yourself to something in a way that overcomes resistance and fear is to take baby steps. First, identify something, or multiple things, you are avoiding. Then, identify what steps or actions involved in this situation that you are feeling resistant to doing. This could be having a conversation, committing to something, taking an action, making an investment, etc. For each of the aspects that you feel resistance about, rate them on a scale of 1 to 10, 10 being extremely high resistance or fear. Put the different aspects or steps in order based on their score. Then, start taking the steps with the lowest level of resistance first, working your way up to the more difficult steps. Doing this builds confidence, and because the smaller tasks are already out of the way, you will feel less overwhelmed and will build your way to the more difficult steps.

Another way to use exposure hierarchies is the exposure ladder. We've included a bonus section, which is coming up next, that shows how to use an exposure ladder to overcome fear of public speaking. The process applies to anything you want to overcome.

Play the Script Until the End (the Worst-Case Scenario): Another great process for overcoming fear and resistance is to actually face the fear itself. The way you do this is to imagine the situation and play the script all the way to the end, which would be the worst case scenario that you are afraid of. The benefit of doing this is that you can see what it would actually be like without having to experience it in real life. It gives you a safe place to see how it would feel and determine how you would cope with it. See the De-Catastrophizing section for an activity.

For other workbooks and the online courses that accompany them,
visit www.transformationacademy.com.

Made in the USA
Middletown, DE
16 October 2023

40848927R00077